16th October 2003.

THE *NEW* COLOUR PICTURE
DICTIONARY

Ages 5 – 9

**Over 1,000 words defined and more than
600 pictures in full colour.**

To

Our wonderful Son, Nic, Happy

7th Birthday Sweetheart, we

love you <u>so</u> much, and we are

<u>very</u> proud of you!! With

All Our Love from your

Mom + Dad

xxx   xxx

xx   xx

xx   x

x

Aa

A is the first letter of the alphabet.
A dog is an animal.
Digger is a dog.

ABLE

You are able to read this book.
Babies are not able to read.
Able means that you can do something.

ABOUT

Digger Dog is about to have his supper.
Digger is going to have his supper very soon.

ABOVE

Billy Budgie flies above the baby's head.
Look above the baby's head to see him.

ACCIDENT

Uncle Harry has had an accident
He has fallen down the stairs.

ACTIVE

Elly Elephant is very active.
She is busy cleaning her trunk.

ADD

Can you add?
2 + 2 = 4
4 + 4 = 8
When you add 4 and 2, you have 6.

ADDRESS

This is Bertie Bear's address
This is where he lives.

ADMIT

Two tickets will admit Daffy Duck and Lucy Lamb to the circus. They can sit at the ringside.

ADVANCE

Look at all these ants as they advance
They all move forward.

ADVENTURE

An adventure is an exciting or unusual event.
Peter had a ride in a helicopter.
That was an adventure

ADVERTISE

People advertise things to sell.
They put notices in newspapers and shop windows.
This is called an advertisement

ALARM

A loud or sudden noise **alarms** us.
We think something may be wrong.
Andy Ambulance sounds an **alarm**
as he speeds on his way.

ALARM CLOCK

The bell on an **alarm clock** rings
to signal to us that it is time to
get up.

ALBATROSS

An **albatross** is a
very large, web-footed
seabird.
An **albatross** can fly long
distances.

ALBUM

An **album** is a book with blank
pages for holding photographs,
pictures or stamps etc.
Annie Antelope has an **album** of
autographs.

AGO

Years **ago** there were no motor cars
or trucks.
In past years people had horses and
carriages.

AGREE

Daniel Dwarf and Eric Elf **agree**.
They do not argue. They think alike.

AIR

We breathe **air**.
Air is all around us.
We cannot see **air** but, when the
wind blows, we feel the **air** moving.
Eddy Eagle flies in the **air**.

AIRCRAFT

An **aircraft** is a machine that flies
through the air.
Arnold **Aircraft** flies high in the
sky.

AIRLINE

Arnold Aircraft carries passengers
for a famous **airline**

AIRPORT

An **airport** is a place where aircraft
take off and land.

AJAR

Albert Ape left the door **ajar**
The door is slightly open.

ALMOST

It is **almost** time to go to bed.
It is nearly bedtime.
Ninety-nine is **almost** one hundred.

ALONE

One boy stood **alone** on the hill.
One girl **alone** can do this puzzle.
She can do it on her own.

ALPHABET

This is a group of letters used in writing a language.
The English **alphabet** is -
A B C D E F G H I J K L M N O
P Q R S T U V W X Y Z .

ALPINE

Alpine plants grow on high mountains like the Swiss **Alps**. **Alpine** skiers ski down high mountains.

AMBITION

Arnold Aircraft's **ambition** is to fly round the world.
He hopes to fly round the world one day soon.

AMBULANCE

Andy **Ambulance** carries the sick and injured to hospital as fast as he can.

AMONG

The children quarrelled **among** themselves so the teacher divided the sweets **among** the children.

AMUSE

Adam Apple can **amuse** his friends by rolling up and down the alley.
Everyone laughs at him.
They all have fun.

ANCHOR

An **anchor** grips the sea bottom and so holds a ship in place.

ANCIENT

We saw the ruins of an **ancient** castle.
The castle is very old.
It was built nine hundred years ago.

AND

Annie Antelope **and** Albert Ape are good friends. They like to run **and** jump **and** play.

ANGEL

An **angel** is a messenger from God.
An **angel** is kind and good.

ANOTHER

Eat **another** sweet.
You may eat one more sweet.
Show me **another** kind of sweet.
I want a different kind of sweet.

ANSWER

Who can **answer** the question first?
The girl gave a quick **answer**.
When the telephone rings Polly Parrot will **answer** it.

ANT

An **ant** is a small insect.
Ants live together in large groups called colonies.

ANTELOPE

An **antelope** looks like a small deer with horns. **Antelope** chew the cud.

APRIL

This is the fourth month of the year.
April has thirty days.
April comes after March.

APRON

An **apron** is a garment worn over our clothes to keep our clothes clean.
Benjamin Butcher wears a striped **apron**.

ARCH

An **arch** is curved.
Arches of wedge-shaped stone are often used to support bridges.
A rainbow **arches** across the sky.

ARMCHAIR

An **armchair** is a comfortable chair with side pieces to support your arms or elbows.

ARMY

An **army** is a group of soldiers trained to fight for their country in times of war.
An **army** of ants means a very large number of ants.

AROUND

Ally Alligator crawled **around** the big tree.
The tree measures two metres **around**.

ARROW

Robin Hood shot a silver **arrow** from his bow.

ARTIST

An artist paints pictures.
Albert Ape painted a picture. He is an artist

AS

Sophie is as tall as James.
Sophie and James are equally tall.
As for the little boy, he is much smaller.

ASTRONAUT

An astronaut travels through outer space in a spacecraft.

AT

Jack is at home today.
He is in the house.
Jack goes to bed at nine o' clock.
When it is nine o' clock, he will go to bed.

ATE

The children ate crisps and cake at the party.
The horse ate the grass in his field.
The cat ate the fish in his dish.

ATHLETE

Frankie Frog is an athlete
He can jump very high.
Ossie Ostrich is an athlete
He can run very fast.

ATLAS

An atlas is a book of maps.
You will find a map of your country in an atlas

ATTACH

We are going to attach the tail to our kite.
We shall fasten the tail to the kite.

ATTEMPT

Jack made an attempt to climb the tree. He tried to climb it.

ATTENTION

The children were paying attention to the teacher. They were listening carefully.
The teacher called their attention to the new dictionary.

ATTIC

The space just below the roof in a house is called the attic.
People often store their old things in the attic

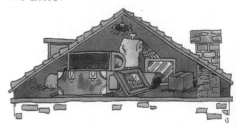

AUDIENCE

Our school play had a large **audience**
All the parents came to see it.

AUGUST

August is the eighth month of the year.
August has thirty-one days.

AUNT

My mother's sister is my **aunt**
My father's sister is my **aunt**
My uncle's wife is my **aunt**, too.

AUTHOR

An **author** is a person who writes books and stories.

AUTOMATIC

An **automatic** kettle turns itself off when the water has boiled.
An **automatic** washing machine will wash and rinse clothes by itself.

AUTUMN

A year is divided into four seasons.
Autumn is the season between summer and winter.

AVENUE

An **avenue** is a wide street with trees on both sides.
Rose lives on Park **Avenue**.

AVERAGE

Joe is an **average** boy.
He is like most boys.
An **average** day is an ordinary day when nothing special happens.

AVOID

Jenny has a cold.
She tries to **avoid** other people when she has a cold.
She stays away from them.

AWAKE

Bouncing Baby is wide **awake**
He is not asleep.

AWAY

Father is **away** today.
He is not near.
The astronaut was far **away** from home.

AWFUL

There was an **awful** storm with thunder and lightning.
It was a dreadful storm.
Tom had an **awful** dream.
It was a very bad dream.

AXE

Farmer Brown chops wood with an **axe**.

Bb

BABY
A **baby** is a very young child.
Bouncing **Baby** is not very old.

BACK
Bertie Bear is riding on Hobby
Horse's **back**.
The **back** of something is the part
behind, like the **back** of this book.

BADGE
A **badge** is a small sign worn on
your clothes to show who you are or
to which group you belong.
Nice Nurse wears a **badge** on her
apron.

BADGER
Brock **Badger** lives in a cosy,
underground
burrow. He has
a white
face with
two
black
stripes.

BARBEQUE
Piggles Pig is cooking his dinner on
a **barbeque** outside in the open
air.

BARBER
Barry **Barber's** business is cutting
hair. He is trying to cut Dolly
Donkey's tail but she keeps swishing
it about.

BARGE
A **barge** is a large, flat-bottomed
boat that sails on rivers and inland
waterways.

BARK
Digger Dog has a loud **bark**.
He likes to **bark** at Clarence Cat.

BARREL
A **barrel** is a round container with
flat ends.
We store things in a **barrel**.
The metal tube of a gun is called
a **barrel**.

BASKET
A **basket** is
a container
made
of sticks or
cane woven
together.
There is a
basket
of fruit on the table.

BAT
Batty **Bat**
looks like a
mouse with
skin-like wings.
He sleeps all day
and flies at night.
When we play
baseball, cricket
and rounders
we
strike
or hit
the
ball
with a
wooden **bat**.

BATHROOM
Look at Peter Penguin having a
bubble bath in the **bathroom**.

BED

Gertie Goat is tired so she has gone to **bed** to have a rest.
We sleep in a **bed**.

BEE

Guess who is making honey.
Yes, it is Buzzy **Bee**.
Watch out, he can sting too!

BEETLE

A **beetle** is a small insect with hard wing-cases.

BEFORE

You should wash your hands **before** you eat.
Two o' clock is earlier than four o' clock. It comes **before**.

BEHAVE

This is the way one acts.
Don't **behave** like a fool.
Act well and do what is right.

BEHIND

Dilly Deer is hiding **behind** a tree.
She is not in front of it.

BELIEVE

I **believe** what you say.
I think you are telling the truth.

BELL

A **bell** is a hollow, metal cup with a clapper that makes a ringing sound when we shake it.

BELONG

These seeds **belong** to Billy Budgie. They are his property.
Does this book **belong** to you?
Do you own it?

BELOW

The basement is **below** the ground floor.
It is underneath it.
The ground is **below** the sky.
The sky is higher than the ground.

BELT

Chief Chef wears a **belt** around his waist to fasten his trousers.

BENCH

You may sit on a **bench** at your local park.
A **bench** is a long, hard seat, usually made of wood or stone.

BENEATH

Clarence Cat is sitting **beneath** the table.
He is sitting underneath the table.

BERTH

A **berth** is a built-up bed on a ship or a train.
Oh dear, Henry Hedgehog has fallen asleep in the Captain's **berth**.

BEST

Gertie Goat likes grass to eat **best** of all.
She prefers grass to any other food.
It is the **best** for her.

BET

I'll **bet** Annie Antelope can run faster than Tilly Tortoise.
Shall we have a **bet** on it?
Watch out, you may lose some money on the wager.

BITE

Digger Dog does not **bite**.
He will not cut you with his teeth.

BITTER

Lemons are **bitter**.
They have a sharp, sour taste.
It is cold because there is a **bitter** wind.

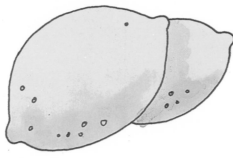

BLACK

Black is a colour.
Caw-Caw Crow has **black**, shiny feathers. You can see him flying round Farmer Brown's farm.

BLACKBOARD

Tommy Teacher uses chalk to write on the **blackboard** at school.

BLUNT

When something is **blunt** it is not sharp.
A **blunt** or dull knife needs to be sharpened to make it cut properly.

BOARD

A **board** is a piece of long, thin, flat wood.

BOAT

A **boat** sails on water.
Flipper Fish has a red **boat**.
When he is tired of swimming around he sunbathes in his **boat**.

BODY

All the parts of a person or animal are its **body**.
Bertie Bear has a strong, healthy **body**.

BOX

My favourite breakfast cereal comes in a **box**.
Aunty Ivy keeps her rings in a **jewel-box**

BOY

Bouncing Baby is a **boy**
He is a male child.
When he grows up he will be a man.

BRACELET

A **bracelet** is a piece of jewellery worn around the arm or wrist.

BRAIN

Your **brain** is in your head.
You think and feel with your **brain**

BRAKE

Your bicycle has a **brake** on it to help you slow it down or stop it.
Whoosh! Minnie Mini-Bus's **brakes** are bad – she can't stop!

BRANCH

Olly Owl and Squeaky Squirrel are having a nap on a tree **branch**.
They are sitting on a limb of the tree.

BRASS

Some musical instruments are made of **brass** – a bright yellow metal.

BRAVE

Olly Owl is **brave**
He is not afraid of the dark.
Policemen are **brave** too.

BREAD

Bread is made of flour, water, yeast and salt.
It is baked in an oven until it is golden brown.

BREAK

Oh dear, poor Spikey Spider!
How did he **break** a leg?
Never mind, he has seven left, he won't miss one!

BREAKFAST

This is the first meal of the day.
Your favourite **breakfast** cereal is in the box on the table.

BREATH

Take a deep **breath**.
Draw air into your lungs and now blow it out.
Your **breath** is the air you take in and let out.

BRIDGE

A **bridge** is built to carry a road, railway or path across a river, road, ravine and so forth.
Bridges are used to cross over something.

BROOK

A **brook** is a small stream.
Sometimes there are lots of fish in a **brook**.

BROTHER

My **brother**, John, and I have the same parents.
John is Jane's **brother**.

BROUGHT

Look what Henrietta Hen has **brought** for her chicks.
She has come with some corn for their supper.

BROWN

Bertie Bear's coat is **brown**.
Brown is a colour.
Chocolates are usually **brown** in colour.

BRUISE

Daniel Dwarf has banged his knee.
He has a **bruise** on his knee.
The **bruise** on his knee turned black and blue.

BRUSH

You should always **brush** your teeth after eating food.
You clean your teeth with a **toothbrush**.
You **brush** your hair with a **hairbrush**.

BUCKET

Jack and Jill used a **bucket** to carry water.

BUCKLE

There will be a **buckle** on your belt.
It is a type of fastener for joining two straps together.

BUD

A **bud** is a flower or leaf before it opens.
This is a **rose-bud**.
There are **buds** on the trees too.

BUDGERIGAR

Billy is a **budgerigar**.
He lives in a lovely cage and sometimes he talks.
Billy **Budgie** is a small, brightly-coloured bird.

BUILD

Hobby Horse needs a new stable.
Will you help to **build** it?
Will you help to make it?
But first, shall we ask Bully
Bulldozer to clear the site?

BULLDOZER

Bully **Bulldozer** is a strong tractor
with a big blade in front.
He pushes soil and other things.

BUN

A **bun** is a small round cake.
Would you like to taste one of
Mother Goose's **buns**.

BUNCH

Bananas
grow in a
bunch.
Mickey
Monkey
has a
bunch of
bananas
in his
hand.

BUNDLE

A **bundle** is a number of things
fastened together.
Brock Badger collects sticks and ties
them into a **bundle** with a piece of
string.

BURN

Do not touch the hot plate, you will
burn your hand.
If you stand too near the fire it will
burn you.

BURY

Digger Dog likes to **bury** his bones.
He digs a hole in the garden and
hides them.

BUS

People ride in a **bus**.
Big **Bus** stops at a **bus-stop** and
picks up passengers.
He is bigger than a car.

BUSH

A **bush** is a small, low tree.
Roses grow on a **bush**.

BUSY

Mother Goose is always **busy**.
She is always working.
She is **busy** all day long.

BUT

But means except or yet.
Daffy Duck's friend loves to swim in
the pond **but**
Clarence Cat does
not like the water.

Cc

CABBAGE
This is a round-shaped vegetable.
Curly **Cabbage** is a green **cabbage**.
Sometimes we eat **cabbage** with our roast beef.

CAKE
Cake is a sweet food baked in the oven.
If you are lucky you will have a birthday **cake** on your birthday.

CALENDAR
A **calendar** lists the months, weeks and days of the year.
A **calendar** shows the day of the week on which each day of the month falls.

CALF
Cassy **Calf** is a baby cow.
She is the daughter of Camilla Cow.

CANOE
A **canoe** is a small, light boat that is propelled by paddles.

CANVAS
Canvas is a heavy, coarse cloth.
Canvas is used for tents and sails and oil paintings.

CAP

Tiggy Tiger likes to wear a **cap** on his head.
A **cap** is a soft hat with a peak at the front which keeps his head warm in cold weather.

CAPITAL
London is the **capital** of England.
Rome is the **capital** of Italy.
A **capital** is the most important city of a country.
What is the **capital** of France?

CAPTAIN

Captain Custard is the person in charge of the ship.
He is the leader.
Johnny is the **captain** of our football team.

CAR
Daddy has a **car**.
A **car** is a motor vehicle.
Sometimes when it is raining he takes me to school in the **car**.

CARAVAN
A **caravan** is a house on wheels which can be pulled by a car or a horse.

CAROL
A **carol** is a religious song sung at Christmas.
Which is your favourite **carol**?

CENTRE

There are two holes near the **centre** of a button.
They are in the middle of the button.
The **centre** of something is the middle.

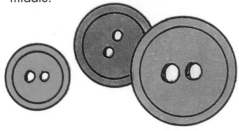

CEREAL

Cereal is a breakfast food made from grain crops such as wheat, rice or maize.
Henrietta Hen likes to eat **cereals**.

CHAIN

Digger Dog has a **chain** around his neck.
A **chain** is a string of metal rings joined together.

CHAIR

A **chair** is something we sit on.
Bouncing Baby sits in a **high-chair** to eat his meals.

CHALK

Tommy Teacher writes on the blackboard with **chalk**.
Chalk is a stick of soft rock with which to write.

CHALLENGE

Tilly Tortoise said to the hare, "I **challenge** you to a race!"
Tilly thought she could beat the hare because in the fable by Aesop the tortoise beat the hare.
Do you know the story?

CHAPTER

A **chapter** is part of a book.
Each section of this book is a **chapter**.
This 'C' section is a **chapter**.

CHART

A **chart** is a special kind of map.
Sailors use **charts** to navigate. The weatherman looks at a weather **chart** to tell us about the weather.

CHEAP

Cheap things do not cost a lot of money.
They are low in price.
They are not dear.

CHEAT

You must not **cheat**.
You must always be honest in your work or play.
Nobody likes to play games with someone who **cheats**.

CHEEK

This is the side of your face.
Cheeks are the fleshy parts on either side of your face under your eyes.
Bouncing Baby has dimples in his **cheeks**.

CHEESE

This is a savoury food made from milk.

Missy Mouse likes to eat **cheese**.

CHEF

Chief **Chef** is a cook.
He is the head cook at the school.
He is the person in charge of cooking.

CINEMA

We go to the **cinema** to watch films in public.
It is usually a large building with rows of seats which all face a big screen.

CIRCLE

This is a **circle**.
It is a perfectly round ring.

CLIFF

A **cliff** is a high, steep rock face near the sea.
Do not go near the edge.
It can be dangerous.

CLIMB

Watch Clarence Cat, he is trying to **climb** the tree.
Watch him go up the tree.

CLOCK

We look at a **clock** to see what time it is.
What time does this **clock** say?

CLOSED

The Post Office is **closed** on Sundays.
It does not open on Sundays.
When the door is **closed** we cannot go inside.

COAT

It is cold outside.
Put on your **coat** to keep warm.
When an animal has beautiful fur, we say it has a beautiful **coat**.

COBWEB

Spikey Spider spins a silken **cobweb** to catch flies. It is made of sticky thread.

COCONUT

A **coconut** is a large, hairy nut that grows on palm trees.
The centre is filled with milky juice.

COIN

This is a piece of money made of metal.
How many **coins** do you have in your piggy bank?

COLT

A young, male horse is a **colt**, whereas a young, female horse is called a filly.

COMPASS

A **compass** is an instrument for showing directions.
The needle of a **compass** always points to the magnetic north pole.

COMPUTER

A **computer** is an electronic machine that stores and processes large amounts of information at great speed.

CONDUCTOR

A **conductor** is the leader of a band.
A bus **conductor** collects fares.

COPY

Can you **copy** this picture of Andy Ambulance?
Can you make a picture that looks the same?

CORNER

Little Jack Horner sat in the **corner**.
A **corner** can be where two streets meet.

CORRECT

To **correct** mistakes is to make right the errors.
Tommy Teacher has to **correct** your homework.

CORRIDOR

This is a long, narrow passage off which rooms open.
There will be several **corridors** at your school.
You must not run down a **corridor**.

COST

The **cost** is the price paid for something.
Do you know the **cost** of this book?

COTTAGE

A **cottage** is a small house.
Mother Goose lives in a thatched **cottage**.

COTTON

Cotton is a soft, white, woolly substance that can be used to make thread.
It comes from the **cotton** bush which grows in warm areas.
Belinda Ballerina's dress is made of **cotton**.

COUNT

To **count** is to add up.
Can you **count** from 1 to 100?
Can you say the numbers in order?
You can **count** on me means you can rely on me.

COUNTRY

Farmer Brown lives in the **country** not the town.

COUSIN
Your **cousin** is the child of your aunt or uncle.
Jane and Jill are **cousins**.

COVER
Please **cover** Bouncing Baby with a blanket.

Please put a blanket over him to keep him warm.

COW
Camilla is a **cow**.
We get milk from a **cow**.

COWBOY

A **cowboy** rides a horse and looks after cattle on a ranch.
There are many **cowboys** in America.

CRAB
A **crab** is a type of shellfish with eight legs and two claws.

CRASH

What a **crash**!
What a loud noise!
Tracy Train has **crashed** into the buffers at the station.

CRAYON

This is a coloured wax-stick or coloured pencil.
We colour pictures with **crayons**.
Can you **crayon** a colourful picture for Mummy?

CREAM
We get **cream** from the milk of Camilla Cow.
Cream is also used to make butter and is a pale yellow colour.

CROCODILE
Christopher **Crocodile** is a large river animal with a long nose, a thick skin, big teeth and short legs.

CROSSING
There is a **crossing** outside your school so that you can **cross** the road safely.

CROW
Caw-Caw **Crow** is a large bird with shiny, black feathers.

He has a loud, harsh voice that says "Caw! Caw!"

CROWN

On important occasions the Queen wears a **crown** on her head. It is a circle of gold with jewels around it.

CRY

Bouncing Baby is **crying** because he is hungry.
We shed tears when we **cry**.

CUCUMBER

A **cucumber** is a long, green vegetable, usually eaten raw with a salad.

CUPBOARD

This is a piece of furniture with shelves inside on which to store things.
Mummy keeps cereals in a **cupboard**.

CURRENT

A **current** is a flow of air or water. The river has a rapid **current**.
A **current** is also a flow of electricity through a wire.

CURTAINS

We hang **curtains** at our windows. The **curtains** at a theatre are wide enough to go across the whole stage.
Curtains are usually made of cloth.

CURVE

A **curve** is not straight.
There is a **curve** in the road.
There is a bend in the road.

CUSHION

This is a soft pillow on which you can sit.
A **cushion** in a chair makes it more comfortable.

CUSTOMER

A **customer** is the person who buys something from a shop.
Benjamin Butcher is telling a **customer** how good the beef is today.

CUT

Bouncing Baby has **cut** a new tooth. A new tooth has come out through his gum. A **cut** is also a small wound. We **cut** things into pieces with a pair of scissors, a knife or a saw.

CUTLERY

We eat our food with **cutlery**. Knives, forks and spoons are **cutlery**.

CYCLE

Farmer Brown will **cycle** after Goosey Gander. He will ride his bicycle as fast as he can to catch naughty Goosey Gander.

23

Dd

DAD
Dad is the name for father.
I call my father **Dad**.
Sometimes I call him **Daddy**.

DAFFODIL
A **daffodil** is a plant with a yellow, trumpet-shaped flower and long, slender leaves.
Dainty Doll dances around a clump of **daffodils**.

DANGER
Beware! If you are in **danger** you may get hurt.
When the light for the traffic is red, and the traffic has stopped, we can cross the street without **danger**.

DAY
A **day** is divided into 24 hours.
There are 7 **days** in a week.
The first **day** of the week is Sunday.

DECEMBER
This is the twelfth and last month of the year.
The date of Christmas Day is **December** 25th.

DEER
Dilly **Deer** is a graceful, wild animal.
A father **deer** is called a buck.
A mother **deer** is called a doe.
A baby **deer** is called a fawn.

DELIVER

The postman **delivers** letters to our houses.
He brings letters to our houses.
Eddy Eagle will **deliver** his party invitations.
He will give them out.

DESK
A **desk** is a table at which we can write, read and draw. It often has drawers in which paper can be kept.
Daniel Dwarf is sitting at his **desk** reading his dictionary.

DESSERT

We eat **dessert** at the end of a meal.
Would you like apple pie, fruit or ice-cream for **dessert**?

DEW
Dew is formed at night on the cool grass.
The grass had small drops of water on it this morning.

DIARY

Bobby Boy writes things in his **diary**.
Doc Doctor has a large **diary** in which he keeps a daily record of his work.

DICTIONARY

A **dictionary** is a book of words from A to Z in alphabetical order.
This book is a **dictionary**.
A **dictionary** tells us the meaning of words.

DIFFERENT

Timmy Tank is **different** from Andy Ambulance.
The two vehicles are not the same.
They are not alike.

DIFFICULT

This trick is **difficult**.
It is hard to do.

DIG

Digger Dog will **dig** a hole with his claws.
He likes to **dig** deep holes to bury his bones.

DINNER

Dinner is our main meal of the day.
At our house we have **dinner** at six o'clock in the evening.

DINOSAUR

A **dinosaur** is one of a group of extinct reptiles.
Some **dinosaurs** were bigger than Elly Elephant and some **dinosaurs** were smaller than Clarence Cat.

DIRECTION

In which **direction** did Arnold Aircraft go?
Did he go north, south, east or west?

DIRTY

Mickey Monkey washed his hands because they were **dirty**.
His hands were not clean.

DISAPPEAR

The sun will **disappear** behind a cloud.
It will go out of sight.
You will not be able to see it.

DISH

A **dish** is something we use to hold food.
We eat from **dishes**. Cups, saucers, plates and bowls are **dishes**.

DIVIDE

Tommy Teacher will **divide** the sweets between the children.
He will share the sweets between them.
They will each get some sweets.

DO

Do your work well.
Your teacher will be pleased if you **do** your best.
When you **do** something you carry out some action or task.

DOCTOR

A **doctor** is a person who takes care of your health.
A **doctor** knows how to treat diseases.
When I am ill **Doc Doctor** comes to examine me.

DOG

A **dog** is an animal.
Digger is a pet **dog**.
Digger is a clever **dog**.
He can do difficult tricks.

DOLL

A **doll** is a toy.
Dainty **Doll** looks just like a little girl.

DONKEY

A **donkey** is an animal that looks like a small horse.
A **donkey** has long ears and a tuft of hair at the end of its tail.
Dolly **Donkey** says, "Hee-Haw."

DOOR

A **door** opens or closes the entrance to a building or a room.
Dad opened the front **door**.

DOT

A **dot** is a small round spot.
At the end of this sentence there is a **dot**.
There are blue **dots** on Dainty Doll's dress.

DOUBLE

To **double** is to make two of something.
John's cake is **double** the size of mine.
If a person looks just like you we say he is your **double**.

DOUBT

I **doubt** Jim's story.
I am not sure it is true.

DRESS

Dainty Doll wears a polka-dot **dress**.
Belinda Ballerina wears a **dress** too.
I can **dress** myself means I can put my clothes on.

DRILL

A **drill** is a tool which makes holes in wood or metal.
To **drill** is to practise. When we have a fire **drill** we practise how to get out of the building.

DRINK

When we **drink** we swallow a liquid.
Watch Bouncing Baby **drink** his milk.
We **drink** when we are thirsty.

DRIP

To **drip** means to fall in drops.
Rain **drips** from the trees.
Water was **dripping** from the tap.
The spilt lemonade **dripped** from the edge of the table.

DRIVE

Farmer Brown can **drive** the tractor.
He can make the tractor go.
Father will **drive** the nail in.
He will hammer the nail into the wood.

DROP

A **drop** is a small amount of liquid in a round shape.
A **drop** of rain fell on my nose.
To **drop** something is to let it fall.

DROWN

If you go into deep water you may **drown**.
If you are under water and cannot breathe you will die.

DRUM

A **drum** is a musical instrument.
Bouncing Baby beats his **drum** with his hands.
Baby Brother beats his **drum** with sticks.

DULL

The knife is **dull**.
It is not sharp.
Yesterday was a **dull** day.
It was not clear and bright.

DUMB

The teddy bear is **dumb**.
He is not able to speak.

DUMP

The men **dump** the rubbish into the big truck.
The rubbish will be taken to a **dump** to be burned.

DURING

Bouncing Baby slept **during** the storm.
He slept while it was going on.

DUST

The rug is full of **dust**
It is full of tiny bits of dirt.
Buzzy Bee is covered with pollen, the yellow **dust** from flowers.

DUTY

A **duty** is an action one ought to do.
Feeding Clarence Cat is Bobby Boy's **duty**.
He has been given that task to do.

DWARF

A **dwarf** is a very small person.
In this book Daniel **Dwarf** is a kind, little man with magic power.

DWELL

Where do you **dwell**?
Where do you live?
Camilla Cow and Cassie Calf **dwell** in the countryside.
They live in the countryside.

DYE

Belinda Ballerina's pink dress is faded.
She can **dye** it red.
She can soak it in **dye** to change the colour.

Ee

EACH

The clown gave **each** of the children a balloon.
He gave every child a balloon.

EAGLE

Eddy **Eagle** is a large bird. He has sharp claws called talons. He sees a long way with his sharp eyes.

EAR

The **ear** is the part of the body used for hearing. Dolly Donkey has long, furry **ears**.
An **ear** is also the word for the seeds at the top of a stalk of corn or wheat.

EAT

When we **eat** we chew and swallow food.
Would you care for something to **eat**?
Camilla Cow and Oscar Ox **eat** grass and grain.

EGG

An **egg** is an oval object laid by birds and some animals.
We eat hens' **eggs**.
Birds, fish, insects, snakes and alligators are born from **eggs**.

EIGHT

Eight is one more than seven.
When you add 4 and 4 you have **8**.
Spikey Spider has **eight** legs.

EIGHTEEN

Eighteen is eight more than ten.
10 and 8 are **18**.
When you add 6 and 6 and 6 you have **18**.

ELEVEN

Eleven is one more than ten.
When you add 10 and 1 you have **11**.

ELSE

Bobby Boy is ill so you must invite someone **else** to the party. Will somebody **else** come? Snowy Snail will come instead of Bobby.
Hurry, Snowy, or **else** you will be late!

EMPLOY

Chief Chef is **employed** to cook meals. He is paid to do this work.

EMPTY

Daffy Duck's handbag is **empty**. There is nothing in it.
Bouncing Baby drank all his milk and his bottle is **empty** now.

ENVELOPE

An **envelope** is a paper cover for a letter, or papers, to be sent in the post. On the front of the **envelope** we write the name and address of the person to whom we are writing.

EQUAL

We use this word to describe things that are the same in amount, size or value.
The children had **equal** shares of the birthday cake.
A square has four **equal** sides. The sides are all the same.

EQUATOR

The **equator** is an imaginary line around the middle of the earth, halfway between the North Pole and the South Pole.

ERASE

Tommy Teacher will **erase** the writing from the blackboard. He will rub it out with a cloth **eraser**.
We use a rubber **eraser** to **erase** pencil marks.

EVEN

Even means equal or level or smooth.
This road is **even**; there are no hills.
The **even** numbers can be exactly divided by two. 2, 4, 6, 8, 10 are **even** numbers.

EVENING

This is the end of the day between sunset and bedtime.
Baby Brother goes to bed early in the **evening**.

EVENT

An **event** is something that happens or takes place.
Bouncing Baby's party is a happy **event**.

EVERY

Every raindrop is wet. All raindrops are wet.
Every bird has feathers. Each one has feathers.

EXCEPT

Chief Chef works every day **except** Sunday. He has a holiday on Sunday.

EXCHANGE

Tommy Teacher asked two girls to **exchange** places. He asked them to change places with each other. We **exchange** presents with our friends at Christmas.

EXCITED

Daffy Duck and Lucy Lamb are **excited** about the visit to the circus. They are filled with delight at the thought of it.

EXCUSE

Snowy Snail has a good **excuse** for arriving late.
"Please **excuse** me," he says. "I'm sorry, but I cannot move any faster."

EXERCISE

We need **exercise** to keep our bodies and minds healthy. When we run we **exercise** our legs. Swimming is an excellent form of **exercise**.

EXHAUSTED

Goosey Gander was **exhausted** after running from Farmer Brown. He was tired out so he went to bed early.

EXIT

The **exit** is the way to go out. Tommy Teacher's school has seven **exits**.

EXPAND

A balloon will **expand** if it is filled with air. It will get bigger.

EXPECT

We **expect** sunny days in summer. When the clouds become dark we **expect** rain.
We think that it will happen.

EXPENSIVE

Belinda Ballerina has a very **expensive** dress. It cost a lot of money.

EXPLAIN

I do not know this word.
The dictionary will **explain** it.
The dictionary will tell what the word means.

EXPLODE

The firework will **explode**. It will break into pieces with a loud bang. Fireworks must be treated with care because they **explode**.

EXPRESS

Baby Brother tried to **express** his idea clearly. He tried to tell us so that we could understand it.
An **express** train is a very fast train.

EXTEND

We **extend** our hands. We hold them out to shake hands with our friends.
If we **extend** something, we make it longer.

EXTRA

This means more than you would normally need or have.
Bobby Boy had an **extra** ice-cream. Tommy Teacher gave the children **extra** time to finish their work.

EYE

An **eye** is the part of the body with which we see. We have two **eyes**. The hole in a needle and the little spots on potatoes are called **eyes**.

Ff

FACE
The front part of your head is your **face**.
Felicity Fairy has a pretty **face**.

FACT
A **fact** is something that is known to be true or to have happened.
It is a **fact** that birds lay eggs.
It is a **fact** that Columbus discovered America in 1492.

FACTORY
A **factory** is a building in which things are made, usually with the help of machines and special tools.
Cars are made in a **factory**.

FADE
When something **fades** it loses its colour or brightness. Washing made Belinda Ballerina's dress **fade**.
When the sun sets, daylight will **fade**.

FAIL
If you **fail** to do something you do not succeed. You are not able to do it.
Elly Elephant will try to dance on her toes but I think she will **fail**.

FAIR
Dainty Doll has **fair** hair. She has light-coloured hair.
The weather is **fair** today. It is clear and sunny.
A **fair** is where people go to show and sell things.

FAIRY
A **fairy** is a tiny, make-believe person in stories. Felicity is a good **fairy** and uses her magic to help human beings.

FAN
A **fan** is something used to stir the air and cool us.
Natalie Niece waves a paper **fan** to cool her face.
Dad cools the room with an electric **fan**.

FAR
Arnold Aircraft has flown **far** away. He is not near; he is a long way off.
Eddie Eagle can see **far**.
Dad's hat is **far** too big for me.
It is much too big for me.

FARE
A **fare** is the money we pay to ride in a public vehicle.
A taxicab has a meter for recording the **fare**.

FAREWELL
We gave Uncle Harry a **farewell** party. He is going on a trip. We all said goodbye and wished him good luck.

FEAR

To **fear** something is to be afraid of something. Some people **fear** snakes.
Most cats **fear** large dogs.
Olly Owl does not **fear** the dark.

FEAST

A **feast** is a rich meal prepared for some special event. Chief Chef prepared a huge **feast** to celebrate Bouncing Baby's birthday. Everyone ate many good things at the party.

FEATHER

A **feather** is very light. Birds are covered with **feathers**. **Feathers** grow out from a bird's skin. Carol Canary has pretty, yellow **feathers**.

FEBRUARY

February is the second month of the year. It has 28 days except in leap years when it has 29 days.
If the last two figures of a year make a number which can be exactly divided by 4, then that year is a leap year.

FILM

A **film** is a moving picture. We can watch a **film** at the cinema or on television. Do you like to watch cartoon **films**?

FINAL

The **final** day of the year is December 31st. It is the last day of the year.
In the word 'final', 'l' is the **final** letter. It comes last.

FIND

Bobby Boy will **find** the lost ball. He is looking for it and will see it.

FINE

A **fine** day is sunny and clear. Tommy Teacher is a **fine** teacher. He is a very good teacher.
Silkworms spin **fine**, soft thread.

FINGER

A **finger** is a part of the hand. Each hand has four **fingers** and one thumb. The **finger** next to the thumb is called the **forefinger** .

FINISH

Baby Brother will **finish** his dinner. He will eat all his dinner.

FIRE

When something is burning we have a **fire**. Beware! **Fire** is hot.
We use a **fire** to keep warm but sometimes a **fire** will burn down a house or a factory.

FIRE-FIGHTER

A **fire-fighter** is a person who is trained to put out fires. A **fire-fighter** belongs to a fire brigade. **Fire-fighters** race to a fire in a fire-engine.

FLAG

A **flag** is a piece of cloth, usually with a pattern or design on it, which is used as the emblem or sign of a country or organisation. Each country has its own **flag**.

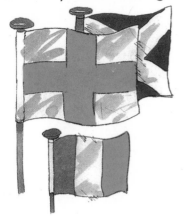

FLAMINGO

A **flamingo** is a large wading bird which lives where the weather is warm. A **flamingo** has a long neck, very long legs and feathers which can vary from pink to bright red.

FLAVOUR

Filly Foal likes the **flavour** of peppermint. She likes the smell and the taste of peppermint. Bobby Boy bought fifteen sweets, each one of which had a different **flavour**.

FLOAT

A boat will **float** on water. It will stay on top of the water and not sink.
A balloon will **float** in the air.

FLOOD

A **flood** is a large amount of water covering what is usually dry land. Heavy rain may cause a river to burst its banks and **flood** the fields.

FLOOR

A **floor** is the bottom part of a room. Bouncing Baby crawls on the **floor**.

FLORIST

A **florist** is someone who grows or sells flowers.
Natalie Niece bought a bunch of flowers from the **florist**.

FLOWER

A **flower** is the blossom of a plant. **Flowers** produce seeds. There are many different kinds of **flowers**. Many **flowers** have a lovely smell and are pretty to look at.

FORK

A **fork** is a piece of cutlery. We use a **fork** to pick up food from our plates. A **fork** has a long handle and two or more prongs for holding the food.

FORTY

Forty is a number.
If you add 20 and 20 you have **40**.
$4 \times 10 = 40$.

FOSSIL

A **fossil** is the hardened remains or impression of an animal or plant and is found in rock.
Bobby Boy found a **fossil** of a fern in a piece of coal.

FOUND

Bobby boy **found** his ball. If you **find** something that was lost, you have **found** it.

FOUR

Four is a number. **Four** is one more than three. $3 + 1 = 4$.
Filly Foal has **four** legs and **four** hooves.

FOURTEEN

Fourteen is a number. **Fourteen** is four more than ten.
If you add 7 and 7 you get **14**.

FOWL

A **fowl** is a bird. Henrietta Hen is a **fowl** and lays eggs for us to eat.

FOX

A **fox** is a wild animal which looks a little like a dog.
Freddy **Fox** has a red, furry coat and a bushy tail.

FREEZE

When the weather is very cold the pond will **freeze**. The water will turn to ice. It is very dangerous to try and walk on a **frozen** pond.

FRIDAY

Friday is the sixth day of the week.
Friday is the day after Thursday and the day before Saturday.

FRIEND

Eric Elf is Daniel Dwarf's **friend**. He likes him very much.
Bobby Boy has many **friends**. He invited all his **friends** to his birthday party.

FRIGHT

When something suddenly scares you it gives you a **fright**.

FROG

A **frog** is a small, wild, leaping creature which lives both on land and in the water. Frankie **Frog** has strong back legs and can jump a long way.

FRONT

The part of anything that faces forward is the **front**. Your nose is on the **front** of your face. Daffy Duck and Lucy Lamb sit in **front** seats when they visit the circus.

FRUIT

A **fruit** is the part of some plants that contains seeds. Apples and oranges are **fruit** but there are many other kinds.
Eating **fruit** is good for your health.

FRY

Mother Goose will **fry** dozens of doughnuts for the party. She will cook them in hot fat or oil in a **frying** pan.

FUEL

This is any substance which can be burned to make a fire. Oil, coal and wood are **fuels**.

Gg

GAIN
Bouncing Baby will **gain** weight as he grows. His weight will increase.

GALAXY
A **galaxy** is a group of stars in the night sky.
The Milky Way **Galaxy** contains the solar system.

GALE
A **gale** is a very strong wind.
A **gale** blew the branch off the tree.

GALLOP
A **gallop** is a quick run. Filly Foal will **gallop** to the circus. She will run as fast as she can.

GARLIC
This is an onion-like plant.
Garlic has a strong taste and smell and is used in cooking.
Do you like the taste of **garlic**?

GARMENT
A **garment** is any article of clothing.
Belinda Ballerina's favourite **garment** is her beautiful, red dress.

GAS
A **gas** is a substance like air.
There are many different **gases** and some burn. We use **gas** for cooking and heating.

GASP
People often **gasp** when they get a surprise or a fright. They take a sudden, short breath.
The members of the audience all **gasp** when they watch Batty Bat, the acrobat, perform on the tight-rope.

GATE
A **gate** is the part in a wall or a fence that opens to let us through.
A **gate** is like a door.
Digger Dog will escape from the garden if you forget to close the **gate**.

GATHER
Natalie Niece will **gather** some flowers. She will pick some flowers. Squeaky Squirrel will **gather** nuts in the autumn. He will collect the nuts together in one place as food for the winter.

GEM
A **gem** is a precious stone or jewel. Diamonds, rubies, emeralds and sapphires are **gems**.

GENTLE
Filly Foal is a **gentle**, little horse. She is quiet and tame.
Digger Dog is a **gentle** dog. He is kind and friendly.

GIANT

A **giant** is a person or thing that is big and strong.
Geoffrey **Giant** is a huge man.
There are **giant**, redwood trees in California.

GIFT

Daffy Duck gave Sammy Seal a **gift**. She gave him a present.

GIRAFFE

A **giraffe** is a very tall animal from Africa with a long neck and spotted skin. George **Giraffe** eats leaves from tall trees.

GIRL

Natalie Niece is a **girl**. She is a female child. When she grows up she will be a woman.

GIVE

Daffy Duck likes to **give** presents to her friends.
If someone **gives** you something you do not have to pay for it.

GLAD

Digger Dog is **glad** that he found his bone. He is happy that he found the bone.
Sammy Seal was **glad** to see all his friends at the party.

GLASS

This is a hard substance which it is easy to break. Light passes through **glass** so window-panes are made of **glass**.
We drink milk from a **glass**.

GLASSES

People who do not see well often wear **glasses** to improve their sight.
Eye **glasses** are made from a special kind of glass.
Dark **glasses** protect our eyes from the sun's rays.

GLIDER

Gilbert **Glider** is an aeroplane without an engine. He **glides** through the sky on currents of air.

GOAT

A **goat** is a domestic animal. The male is called a 'Billy' and has horns and a beard. We get milk from the female or 'Nanny'. Gertie **Goat** is very active.

GOLD

This is a beautiful, precious, yellow metal.
Aunty Ivy has a **gold** ring on her finger. Dad has a watch made of **gold**.

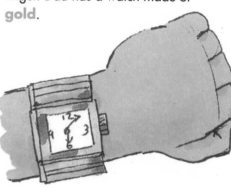

GOLDFISH

Gilly **Goldfish** is a small gold-coloured fish. She lives in a glass bowl.

GOLF

Golf is an outdoor game, played on a special course, in which a small, solid ball is hit with sticks called clubs into a series of holes.

GOOSE

A **goose** is a large bird that can swim. A **goose** looks a little like a duck but it has a longer neck. The meat of **geese** is good to eat.

GRAND

This means great, splendid or important.
Kings and queens often live in **grand** palaces.

GRANDCHILD

Someone's **grandchild** is the child of that person's daughter or son. You are the **grandchild** of your grandparents.

GRANDFATHER

Your father's father is your **grandfather**.
Your mother's father is also your **grandfather**.

GRANDMOTHER

Your mother's mother is your **grandmother**.
Your father's mother is your **grandmother** too.

GRAPE

A **grape** is a small, round fruit that grows in bunches on a vine.
A **grape** is red, purple or pale green.
Grapes can be made into wine.

GRAPEFRUIT

A **grapefruit** is a round, yellow, sour fruit, like an orange but larger.

GRASS

Grass is a plant with long, narrow, green leaves. **Grass** grows on a lawn or in fields. Some animals eat **grass**.

GRASSHOPPER

A **grasshopper** is an insect with strong, long legs for jumping.

GREAT

This means large or important.
Mount Everest is a **great** mountain. The Olympic Games are a **great** sporting event.

GREEDY

Please do not be **greedy**.
If you are a **greedy** person you want more than your share.

GREEN

Green is a colour.
In summer the leaves of the trees are **green**.

GREET

Sammy Seal will **greet** his friends when they come to his party.
He will give them a warm welcome.

GREY

Grey is a colour.
Elly Elephant has **grey** skin.
Dolly Donkey has a **grey**, furry coat.

GRILL

When we **grill** food we place it on a metal frame to cook under the source of the heat.

GRIND

To **grind** means to crush into small pieces or into powder.
The grocer will **grind** the coffee beans in a **grinder**.

GROCER

A **grocer** is a person who sells food.
Mother Goose went to the **grocer's** shop to buy coffee, sugar and flour.

GUARD

A **guard** watches against danger to people or property. A **life-guard** keeps us safe at the swimming pool or beach.

GUESS

Can you **guess** the number of sweets in the jar?
Can you think of the right number?

GUEST

A **guest** is a visitor at your home.
There were many **guests** at Sammy Seal's party.

GUST

A sudden, strong rush of air is called a **gust**.
A **gust** of wind blew Dainty Doll's umbrella inside out.

GUY

A **guy** is a rope or chain to steady or hold something in position – as the ropes on a tent do.

GYMNASIUM

A **gymnasium** is a large room fitted out with special apparatus where people exercise to keep fit and healthy.

GYMNASTICS

Gymnastics are exercises for strengthening the body.
A **gymnast** is a person who is an expert in **gymnastics**.

Hh

HABIT
A **habit** is a thing that you do almost without thinking because you have done it so often.
Brushing your teeth is a good **habit**.

HAD
This bottle **had** milk in it but it does not have any in it now. Baby Brother **had** a kite but it flew away. He owned a kite but he does not have it now.

HADDOCK
A **haddock** is a sea-fish that is good to eat. A **haddock** is like a cod but smaller.

HAIR
Hair grows on the heads and bodies of animals and people.
Hair is like fine threads.
Hair on most animals is called fur.

HANDLE

We hold things by the **handle**.
Cups, cutlery, doors, hammers, pails and suitcases all have **handles**.
If you **handle** something you touch it with your hand.

HANDSOME
Handsome means good-looking.
We usually say that men and boys are **handsome**.

HANG

When we **hang** something we fasten it at the top and let it swing freely at the bottom.
We **hang** our clothes in a wardrobe.
Dad will **hang** his hat on a hook.

HARP
A **harp** is a large musical instrument with strings that are stretched across its frame and played with the fingers.

HARVEST
Harvest is the time or season when the ripe crops are gathered in.
To **harvest** is to reap and collect the crops which are ready.

HAS
Dainty Doll **has** an umbrella.
She owns an umbrella.
The jar **has** sweets in it.
The jar contains sweets.

HAT

A **hat** is worn on the head to keep it warm or to protect it.
Bouncing Baby wears a woollen **hat**.
A fireman wears a hard **hat**.

HATCH

To **hatch** means to break out of an egg to be born. Birds, fish, snakes and insects **hatch**.
A ship's **hatch** is the opening in the deck through which the cargo is loaded.

HAVE

To **have** means to hold or to own or to experience.
I **have** a ball in my hand.
I **have** a gold ring.
I **have** a good time at parties.

HAWK

A **hawk** is a bird with a hooked beak and strong, curved claws.
A **hawk** hunts and eats small birds and animals.

HAY

Hay is dried grass that is used to feed horses and cattle.

HEAR

You **hear** sounds with your ears.
Did you **hear** the music?
Did you listen to it?

HEART

The **heart** is the part of the body that pumps blood round the body.
The **heart** of a thing is the centre or main part of it.

HEAT

Heat is the feeling of warmth that comes from the sun or a fire or a radiator.
When we **heat** something we make it warm or hot.

HEAVY

Things that weigh a lot are **heavy**.
Heavy things are hard to lift.
Elly Elephant is very **heavy**.

HEIGHT

Height is how tall someone is or how high something is.
We measure **height** from the ground upwards.

HELP

To **help** is to make things easier for someone else by doing something useful.
Gracie Gosling will **help** Mother Goose bake the cakes.

HEMISPHERE

Half of a sphere or half of the Earth's surface is called a **hemisphere**.
Our Earth can be divided into Eastern or Western **Hemispheres**, or into Northern and Southern **Hemispheres**.

HEN

A **hen** is a female bird.
A **hen** lays eggs.
When the eggs hatch the **hen** takes care of the chicks.

HER

Her means belonging to a girl, a woman or a female animal.
Dainty Doll has lost **her** umbrella.
Filly Foal will let you stroke **her** head.

HERD

A **herd** is a number of animals together.
Farmer Brown has a large **herd** of cows and a small **herd** of goats.

HERE

Here is the place where you are at this time.

HID

Digger Dog **hid** his bone in a hole in the ground.
He put his bone out of sight.

HIGH

The kite flew **high** into the air. It flew a long way above the ground.
A mountain is **high**. It is a long way from the bottom to the top.

HILL

A **hill** is a piece of ground that is higher than the ground around it but not as high as a mountain.

HOLE

A **hole** is a hollow place, or an opening, or a gap made in something.
There is a **hole** in the fence.
Bobby Boy has a **hole** in his shoe.
Reginald Rabbit lives in a **hole** in the ground.

HOLIDAY

A **holiday** is a day, or days, of rest from school or work.
Christmas is a **holiday** for many people.

HOLLOW

If a thing is **hollow** it has an empty space inside it. It is not solid.
Many rubber balls are **hollow**.
A **hollow** is also a kind of hole.

HOME

The place where you live is your **home**.
A hive is Buzzy Bee's **home**.
A cave is Batty Bat's **home**.

HOMEWORK

Homework is the work that you bring from school to do at home.

HONEST

Bobby Boy is an **honest** boy. He never cheats or steals or tells lies. Everyone likes him because he can be trusted.

HONEY

Honey is the sweet, sticky food that bees make from the drops of nectar they collect from flowers.

HOOF

A **hoof** is the hard part of a foot of some animals such as the horse, cow, sheep and pig.
We call the whole of a foot of such animals a **hoof**.

HOOK

A **hook** is a piece of bent metal for catching hold of something or for hanging things on.
You hang your coat on a **hook**.
An angler has a **hook** to catch fish.

HOP

To **hop** is to leap on one foot or to move in jumps like a frog, a bird or a kangaroo.
Kathy Kangaroo can **hop** very far.

HORSE

A **horse** is a strong animal that is used for riding or for pulling carts and carriages.

HORSESHOE

A **horseshoe** is a U-shaped, flat piece of metal nailed to the underside of a horse's hoof to protect it.

HOSPITAL

A **hospital** is a place where people who are ill or hurt are cared for.
Nice Nurse works in a **hospital**.

HOT

Fire is **hot**. If a thing is **hot** it is very, very warm. Never touch **hot** things because they will burn you.

HOTEL

A **hotel** is a building where people pay to have meals and a room in which to sleep when they are away from home.

HOUR

An **hour** is a measure of time. One **hour** is sixty minutes.
There are twenty-four **hours** in a day.

HOUSE

A **house** is a building in which people live.

HOW

How is a word which means 'In what way?' or 'To what extent?' or 'In what condition?'
How did the accident happen?
How tall is George Giraffe?
Doc Doctor said, "**How** do you feel today?"

HUG

Mother gave Bouncing Baby a **hug**. She put her arms around him and held him close with a gentle squeeze.

HUGE

Elly Elephant is **huge**. She is very, very big.
Ronnie Rhinoceros is **huge** too. He is very large like Elly.

Ii

I
When you are speaking of yourself you use 'I'.
Bobby Boy said, "I like Digger Dog and he likes me."

ICE
Ice is frozen water. It is hard and cold.
Beware! It is dangerous to skate on thin ice.

ICE-CREAM
Ice-cream is a frozen food that is made from cream, sugar and flavourings. Baby Brother likes chocolate ice-cream.

ICICLE
An icicle is a pointed, hanging spike of ice. Icicles form when dripping water freezes.

IDEA
An idea is a thought or plan you have in your mind.
Dad had an idea for an exciting holiday but he had no idea that it would cost so much.

IDENTICAL

When two or more things are the same in every detail, they are identical.
Identical twins are exactly alike.

IDENTIFY
To identify means to recognise or pick out a certain person or thing.
Aunty Ivy can identify a hyacinth by its smell.

IDLE
Lazy Jack Jaguar is idle.
He is not doing anything.

IF
You may go if it is fine.
You may go provided that it is fine.
If it rains I could take an umbrella.
Supposing that it rains I could take an umbrella.

IGLOO
An igloo is an Eskimo house that is shaped like a dome and made of blocks of hard snow.

IGNORANT
Uncle Harry is ignorant about sailing.
He knows nothing about sailing.

ILL
David is ill.
He has a fever.
He is not well.

ILLUSTRATE

Bobby Boy has written a story.
Now he will **illustrate** it.
He will draw pictures about the story.

IMAGINE

To **imagine** is to create a picture or an idea in your mind.
Baby Brother likes to **imagine** he is an engine driver.

IMPOLITE

Anyone showing bad manners and rudeness to others is **impolite**.
It is **impolite** to be greedy.

IMPORTANT

If something is **important** it is noteworthy.
Mount Everest is an **important** mountain.
Your birthday is an **important** day.

IN

Bertie Bear lives **in** a cave **in** the winter.
Please come **in**; the others will be here **in** a minute.
Digger Dog dug a hole **in** the garden.

INCH

An **inch** is a measure of length.
One **inch** equals 2.4 centimetres.

INCREASE

To **increase** is to make or become bigger.
If Piggles Pig eats much more he will **increase** in size.

INDEED

Belinda Ballerina is **indeed** happy with her new dress.
She is really happy.
George Giraffe is tall; **indeed** he is very tall.
George Giraffe is tall; in fact he is very tall.

INDOORS

You are **indoors** when you are inside a house or another building.
If it rains, Clarence Cat will stay **indoors**.

INFLAMMABLE

When something is **inflammable** it is easily set on fire.
Petrol and matches are **inflammable**.

INFLATE

To **inflate** is to blow or puff air or gas into something to make it swell out.
We **inflate** balloons.

INFORM

Mother will **inform** Tommy Teacher of David's illness.
She will tell him, "David is ill."

INK

Ink is a coloured liquid.
When we write with a pen we use **ink**.
Ink is used in the printing of books, newspapers and comics.

INSECT

An **insect** is a tiny animal with six legs.
Flies, ants, butterflies, gnats, bees and beetles are all **insects**.

INSIDE

Bouncing Baby is **inside** the house.
He is not outside, he is within.
Your brain is **inside** your head.

INTELLIGENT

Intelligent means able to learn and understand things quickly.

INTERESTED

To be **interested** means that you want to know or do something.

Bobby Boy is **interested** in reading and collecting autographs.

INTO

Jontie Jeep will go **into** the garage.
He will go inside the garage.
The wicked witch turned the prince **into** a frog.

INVENT

To **invent** is to design or make or think of something entirely new.
People who **invent** things often become famous.

INVITE

To **invite** is to ask someone politely to do something or to come to some place.
Albert Ape likes parties; will you **invite** him?

IRON

Iron is a hard, strong metal.
Horseshoes are made out of **iron**.
An **iron** is a machine that we heat and use to press the creases out of our clothes.

ISLAND

An **island** is a piece of land with water all round it.

ITCH

An **itch** is the prickly, tickling feeling in your skin that makes you want to scratch yourself.
Gnat bites **itch**.

IVY

Ivy is a climbing, evergreen plant with shiny, dark-green leaves.
Ivy clings to walls and trees by very small roots.

Jj

JACKET
A **jacket** is a short coat.
Farmer Brown wears a **jacket** with large checks.

JAGUAR
A **jaguar** is an animal much like a leopard but larger.
Jack **Jaguar** eats meat and fish. He is a good climber and an excellent swimmer as well.

JAIL
A **jail** is a prison. People who do bad things are sometimes put into **jail**.
A **jail** is a building with bars on the doors and windows.

JAM
Jam is a food made by boiling fruit and sugar together.
Many things crowded together so it is hard to move is called a **jam**.
Big Bus was delayed by a traffic **jam**.

JANUARY
January is the first month of the year.
It has thirty-one days.

JEEP
A **jeep** is a strong, four-wheel drive vehicle.
Jontie **Jeep** can travel safely across hilly country or very rough roads.

JELLY
Jelly is a clear, wobbly food made from fruit juice and sugar.
The children ate orange **jelly** and ice-cream at the party.

JEWEL
A **jewel** is a very valuable and beautiful stone, such as a diamond or a ruby.
Aunty Ivy wears a necklace made of **jewels** and gold.

JOG
To **jog** is to run at a slow, even pace or to shake or push against something with a jerk.
Some people go **jogging** to keep fit.
Please do not **jog** my elbow.

JOIN
To **join** is to fasten things together or to become a member of a group.
We all **join** hands to form a circle.
Batty Bat would like to **join** the circus.

JOINT
A **joint** is the place at which two things are joined together. The elbow is the **joint** between the wrist and the shoulder.

JOKE
A **joke** is something said or done to make people laugh.

JOLLY

Brian Baker is very **jolly**.
He is happy and full of fun.

JOURNEY

A **journey** is a trip.
To **journey** is to travel.
Arnold Aircraft will make a long **journey** round the world.

JOY

Joy is a feeling of great happiness.
Bobby Boy jumped for **joy** when he scored a goal.

JUDGE

The **judge** in a court of law sends people to jail, or makes them pay a fine for doing wrong.
A **judge** can also be a person chosen to settle a quarrel or to decide the winner in a contest.

JUG

A **jug** is a container with a handle and a spout that is used for pouring liquids.

JUICE

Juice is the liquid in fruit, meat and vegetables.
Orange **juice** is sweet.
Lemon **juice** is sour.
We make gravy with meat **juice**.

JULY

July is the seventh month of the year.
July has thirty-one days.

JUMP

To **jump** is to leap or spring into the air. Kathy Kangaroo can **jump** very far.
Filly Foal is too young to **jump** over the high fence.

JUNE

June is the sixth month of the year.
June has thirty days.

JUNGLE

A **jungle** is a dense, over-grown forest in a very hot country.
Jack Jaguar lives in a **jungle** in South America.

JURY

A **jury** is a group of people in a court of law who decide whether a prisoner is guilty or not.
A **jury** can also be a group of people chosen to decide winners in a contest.

JUST

Just means fair and proper.
A judge must give a **just** punishment.
Just means only.
Baby Brother is **just** a small boy.
Just means exactly.
This present is **just** what I wanted.

Kk

KALEIDOSCOPE

A **kaleidoscope** is a toy made from a tube, containing mirrors, in which bits of coloured glass make continually-changing, symmetrical patterns as the end of the tube is turned.

KANGAROO

A **kangaroo** is an Australian animal with strong hind legs for jumping.
A female **kangaroo** has a pouch in front in which she carries her baby.

KAYAK

A **kayak** is an Eskimo canoe made from animal skins stretched over a frame of bones or wood with an opening in the middle for the person to sit in and paddle.

KEEP

If you **keep** something you hold on to it as your own for a long time or forever.
Keep also means to have and take care of.
Farmer Brown **keeps** chickens.

KENNEL

Digger Dog sleeps in a **kennel** in the garden. Digger's little house is cosy and warm.

KERB

The **kerb** is the edge of the pavement or sidewalk next to the road.
It is dangerous to walk too close to the **kerb**.

KETCHUP

Ketchup is a tasty sauce made from tomatoes, mushrooms, sugar, vinegar, salt and spices.
Bobby Boy puts **ketchup** on his hamburger.

KETTLE

We boil water in a **kettle**.
A **kettle** is a pot with a lid, a handle and a spout.

KEY

A **key** is a piece of metal shaped to fit into a lock and used for locking and unlocking.
A **key** is also one of the parts on a typewriter, piano or computer that you press to make it work.

KEYBOARD

A **keyboard** is the set of keys on a piano, typewriter or computer.

KEYHOLE

A **keyhole** is a small opening in a lock into which a key is put to turn the lock.

KICK

When you **kick** something you hit it with your foot.
Bobby Boy will try to **kick** the football into the goal.
Hobby Horse does not **kick**.

KID

A **kid** is a young goat.
Aunty Ivy has a pair of **kid** gloves.
They are made of soft leather.

KILL

To **kill** means to make someone or something die.
Cats **kill** mice.

KILOGRAM

A **kilogram** is a measurement of weight equal to 1,000 grammes or 2.2046 pounds.
How much do you weigh?

KILOMETRE

A **kilometre** is a measurement of distance equal to 1,000 metres or 3280.8 feet.
How far can you swim?

KIMONO

A **kimono** is a long, loose, Japanese robe with wide sleeves.
It is fastened with a sash.

KIND

To be **kind** is to be gentle, friendly and helpful towards others.
A **kind** means a type or sort of a thing.
Which **kind** of ice-cream do you like best?

KING

Some countries have a **king**.
The **king** is the man who rules the country and its people.
A **king** wears a crown on a special occasion.

KIOSK

A **kiosk** is a small, covered stall that sells newspapers, magazines and sweets.
A small building for a public telephone is also called a **kiosk**.

KISS

To **kiss** is to touch people with your lips.
We usually **kiss** the people we love.

KITCHEN

A **kitchen** is a room where food is prepared and cooked.
Chief Chef works in a **kitchen**.

KITE

A **kite** is a toy made of paper or cloth on a light, wooden frame that flies in the wind at the end of a long string.

KITTEN

A **kitten** is a young cat.
When Clarence Cat was a **kitten** he liked to play with Mother's knitting wool.

49

KIWI

The kiwi, a bird of New Zealand, is both tailless and flightless and feeds only at night.
A kiwi fruit is a Chinese gooseberry.

KNEE

Your knee is the joint in the middle of your leg where it bends.

KNEEL

When you kneel you get down on your knees.
Some people kneel to pray.

KNIFE

A knife is a cutting tool with a sharp blade and a handle.

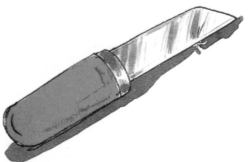

KNIGHT

In days of old a knight was a man in armour who fought on horseback for his king.

KNIT

Natalie Niece will knit a scarf. She will use long needles to weave loops of wool into material.

KNOB

A knob is a round lump at the end of or on the surface of a thing.
A round handle on a drawer or a door is called a knob.

KNOCK

To knock is to hit something either by accident or on purpose.
Please do not knock the dish off the table.
Albert Ape will knock on the door when he arrives at the party.

KNOT

When you fasten your shoelaces you make a knot.
The knot is the twisted part where the laces are tied together.

KNOW

To know is to recognise, or to understand, or to be sure about something.
We know our friends. We know that 3+3 makes 6. We know that water is wet.

KNOWLEDGE

Knowledge is all the information and facts that are known or can be learned.
Your knowledge is all the things that you know now.

KOALA

Katy Koala is a grey, furry, Australian animal like a small bear. She carries her babies in a pouch and feeds only on the leaves of the eucalyptus trees in which she lives.

Ll

LABEL

A **label** is a piece of paper or card-board fastened to a thing telling what or whose it is, or where it is going.

LABORATORY

A **laboratory** is a room or building where scientific work and research are carried out.

LACE

Lace is a fine material with a pretty pattern of holes in it.
Dainty Doll's dress has been trimmed with **lace**.

A **lace** is the thin cord or leather thong used to fasten a boot or shoe.

LAME

Poor Ossie Ostrich is **lame**. He is not able to walk properly because his foot is hurt.

LAMP

A **lamp** gives light when and where we want it.
Street **lamps** come on at dusk.
A lighthouse has a powerful **lamp** that shines across the sea at night.

LAND

Land is the solid part of the Earth's surface that is not covered by water.
To **land** is to come down from the air on to the ground or water.

LANGUAGE

Language is words and sounds used by people when they write and speak.
There are thousands of **languages** but English is the most-used **language**.

LAP

When Mother is sitting down she holds Bouncing Baby on her **lap**.
Once round a race track is a **lap**.

LAWN

A **lawn** is a stretch of grass, usually in a garden, that is kept closely cut.

LAY

Lay means to place or put something down.
Lay your book on the table.
Lay also means to produce an egg.
Birds **lay** eggs.

LAZY

Albert Ape is **lazy**. He does not want to do any work.

LEAD

To **lead** is to go first and show others where to go or what to do.
The strap that fits on to a dog's collar is called a **lead**.

LEAF

A **leaf** is one of the thin, flat, green parts that grow on trees and other plants.

LEAK

A **leak** is a hole or a crack through which liquid or gas passes in or out. A **leak** in a boat lets water get in. Gas can escape through a **leak** in a pipe.

LEAN

To **lean** is to bend over from an upright position toward something. Do you **lean** on your desk at school? Dad will **lean** the ladder against the wall.

LEAP

A **leap** is a big jump.
To **leap** is to spring or jump into the air. Frankie Frog can **leap** very far.

LEG

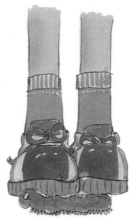

A **leg** is a part of the body.
We stand, walk and run using our **legs**. A person has two **legs**.
Filly foal has four **legs**.
A centipede has many **legs**.

LEMON

A **lemon** is a sour, pale yellow fruit. We make **lemonade** from **lemon** juice, sugar and water.

LEND

To **lend** is to let another have or use for a short time something of yours which they will return.
Will you **lend** me your ladder for today?

LENGTH

Length is how long something is. Measure the distance from one end to the other to find the **length**.

LEOPARD

A **leopard** is a large, wild animal of the cat family that is found in Africa and Asia.
Leonard **Leopard** has dull yellow fur spotted with black.

LESSON

A **lesson** is something that has been or is to be learned.
The time when we are being taught is called a **lesson**.

LETTER

A **letter** is a sign used for writing words. A, B and C are **letters**.
A **letter** is a written message that is put in an envelope and sent to someone.

LETTUCE

A **lettuce** is a vegetable that can be eaten raw in salads.
Letty **Lettuce** has large, crisp, green leaves.

LEVEL

Level means flat and even.
An ice-rink is **level**.

LIBRARY

A **library** is a room or a building where collections of books are kept. Public **Libraries** lend books.

LICK

If you **lick** something you move your tongue over it.
We **lick** lollipops.

LIFE

Life is the time between birth and death.
Life is being alive. People, animals and plants have **life**.

LIFEBOAT

A **lifeboat** is a strong boat built for going out to sea in bad weather to save people from drowning.

LIGHT

Light is a brightness by which we are able to see things.
We get **light** from the sun and from lamps.
Light also means not heavy. Feathers are **light**.

LIGHTHOUSE

A **lighthouse** is a tower topped with a bright light that shines out over the sea at night to warn sailors of danger.

LIKE

If you **like** someone or something you are fond of them.
Do you **like** lollipops?
Like can also mean the same or almost the same as another person or thing.
A wolf is **like** a dog.

LILAC

Lilac is a bush with white or pale purple blossoms that smell very sweet.
The colour **lilac** is pale pink or purple.

LIQUID

A **liquid** can be poured. A **liquid** is wet and flows freely, like water, milk or oil.

LISTEN

When we **listen** we pay attention and make an effort to hear something.
Do you like to **listen** to music?

LITTER

Litter is bits of paper or rubbish left lying about.
A number of young animals born to the same mother at the same time is called a **litter**.

LOCK

A **lock** is a fastening for a door, a gate, a drawer or a box that is opened with its own special key.

LOG

A **log** is a piece of wood cut from the branches or the trunk of a tree. The daily record of the journey of a ship or an aircraft is called a **log**.

LOLLIPOP

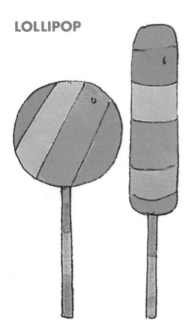

A **lollipop** is a big, hard sweet on the end of a stick.

LONG

This means measuring a lot in length or time. The moon is a **long** way from Earth. A year is a **long** time.

LOOK

To **look** is to turn your eyes in order to see something.
Stop, **look** and listen before you cross the road.

LOST

If something is **lost** you no longer have it.
Bobby Boy **lost** his ball.

LOUD

A **loud** noise is very easy to hear. Caw-Caw Crow has a **loud** voice.

LOVE

If you **love** someone or something you like them or it very, very much. Mother Goose **loves** Gracie Gosling.
Albert Ape **loves** parties!

LOW

Low means not high or tall.
Filly Foal can jump a **low** fence. When Batty Bat is flying **low** he is near the ground.

LUCK

Luck is that which seems to happen or come to us by chance.
Luck can be good or it can be bad.

LULLABY

A **lullaby** is a gentle song that is sung to make a baby fall asleep. Bouncing Baby likes to listen to a **lullaby**.

LUNCH

Lunch is a meal that we eat in the middle of the day.

Mm

MACARONI

Macaroni is thin tubes of wheat-flour paste that we cook and eat.

MACHINE

A **machine** is a thing with several moving parts that work together to do some particular job.
Machines make work easier.
A lawn-mower is a **machine** for cutting grass.

MAGAZINE

A **magazine** is a thin book coming out each week or month with different stories and pictures in it.

MAGNIFY

To **magnify** something is to make it appear larger than it really is.
People use telescopes to **magnify** the stars.

MAIL

Mail is letters, cards or parcels sent by post.
The postman brings us **mail**.
If you **mail** a letter you put it in the **mail-box**.

MAIN

Main means the most important.
Dinner is the **main** meal of the day.

MAKE

To **make** is to create, build or produce something by putting different materials together.
Most birds **make** nests.
Make also means to cause to happen or to amount to.
Do not **make** a noise.
Two and two **make** four.
2+2 = 4.

MANNERS

Manners means our behaviour towards others.
A person with good **manners** is polite.

MAP

A **map** is a flat drawing that shows details of the Earth's surface or some part of it.
Maps help us to find our way.

MARCH

March is the third month of the year.
March has thirty-one days.

MARGARINE

Margarine is a food which looks like butter, although it is made from vegetable oils and animal fats.

MARK

A **mark** is a stain or spot such as dirty **marks** on a clean floor.
A **mark** is the sign that shows what or where a thing is.
A **mark** on a piece of schoolwork is a letter or number to show how well you have done.

MATTER

A **matter** is a thing or job that needs to be thought about or done. Road Safety is an important **matter**.

We say "What is the **matter**?" to find out what is wrong.

MAY

May is the fifth month of the year. **May** has thirty-one days.

MAYBE

Maybe means perhaps or possibly. **Maybe** Bobby Boy will find his ball today.

MAYOR

A **mayor** is the head of a town or city government.

Mr **Mayor** was chosen as the leader by the people who live in the town.

MEDICINE

A doctor gives us **medicine** when we are ill.

Medicine is any liquid or pills that we must swallow in order to get well again.

MEET

To **meet** means to come together or join.

Batty Bat asked Albert Ape to **meet** him at the circus.

MELON

A **melon** is a large, many-seeded fruit with a green or yellow skin. A **melon** grows on a vine.

MELT

To **melt** means to change from a solid to a liquid.

When the ice on a pond **melts**, it is turned into water by the sun's heat.

MEMORY

Memory is the ability to remember. Bobby Boy does not forget things because his **memory** is good. Anything that we remember is called a **memory**.

MEND

To **mend** is to repair a damaged thing to make it useful again. Dad will **mend** the broken toy.

MERRY

Merry means joyful and happy and full of fun.

Did you have a **Merry** Christmas?

MESSAGE

When you send a **message**, you send either spoken or written information to someone elsewhere.

MIDNIGHT

Midnight is twelve o'clock at night.

Midnight is the middle of the night.

MILE

A **mile** is a measurement of length. A **mile** is the distance which is equal to 5,280 feet, 1,760 yards or 1.6092 kilometres.

MILK

Milk is a white, liquid food that we drink and use in cooking.
We get **milk** from cows and goats.
Farmer Brown has to **milk** his cows twice a day.

MIND

Your **mind** is the part of you that knows, thinks, has feelings and decides your actions.
To **mind** is to take care of.
Mind also means to dislike or object to something. Do you **mind** wet weather? Daffy Duck does not **mind** it at all.

MINI-BUS

A **mini-bus** is a small bus. Minnie **Mini-Bus** has fewer seats than Big Bus.

MIST

Mist is a thin fog or a very fine rain through which it is difficult to see.

MISTAKE

A **mistake** is an error or a fault. Tommy Teacher found one **mistake** in Bobby Boy's homework.

MIX

Mix means to mingle or to stir together.
Mother Goose will **mix** butter, sugar, flour, eggs and milk to make a cake.
Bobby Boy and Baby Brother **mix** well with the other children at the party.

MONDAY

Monday is the second day of the week, the day after Sunday.

MONEY

Coins and banknotes are **money**. We buy things with **money**.
Daffy Duck keeps her **money** in her handbag.

MONKEY

A **monkey** is a small animal which lives in trees. Mickey **Monkey** has a long tail and his hands look somewhat like ours.

MONTH

A **month** is a period of time. The year is divided into twelve **months**. They are January, February, March, April, May, June, July, August, September, October, November and December.

MOON

We see the **moon** in the sky at night.
The **moon** moves round the Earth every 29½ days. Sometimes we see all of one side of it; sometimes we only see part of one side. We never see the far side of the **moon** from Earth.
The **moon** appears to shine because it reflects the light of the sun.

MOSS

Moss is a tiny, ground-hugging green plant that grows in tight clusters on moist ground, rocks and trees. Some birds line their nests with **moss** because it is very soft.

MOST

Most means the greatest in number, amount or degree.
Most children like sweets.
Bobby Boy scored the **most** goals.
Ossie Ostrich's foot is **most** painful.

MOTHER

A **mother** is a female parent.
To **mother** is to take care of.
Natalie Niece likes to **mother** Bouncing Baby.

MOTOR

A **motor** is a machine that makes things move.
This lawn-mower is run by a petrol **motor**.

MUD

Mud is soft, wet, sticky earth.
Please wipe the **mud** off your boots.

MUG

A **mug** is a tall cup with a handle.
We drink liquids from **mugs**.

MULE

A **mule** is an animal which is half donkey and half horse.
A **mule** can carry very heavy loads.

MULTIPLY

To **multiply** is to increase in number.
Daisies **multiply** from year to year.
In arithmetic, to **multiply** is to add a number to itself a set number of times.
Two **multiplied** by five equals ten.
$2 \times 5 = 2+2+2+2+2 = 10$.

MUSEUM

A **museum** is a building where collections of valuable and interesting things are on show.
There was a huge skeleton of a dinosaur at the **museum**.

MUSHROOM

A **mushroom** is a fungus that grows very quickly and is good to eat.
Mushy **Mushroom** is shaped like an umbrella.

MUSIC

Music is sound that is pleasing to hear.
We make **music** when we sing or when we play **musical** instruments.

MUST

Must means that you have to or ought to do a certain thing.
Bobby Boy **must** feed Digger Dog every day.
You **must** keep away from dangerous places and dangerous things.

MYSTERY

A **mystery** is something strange that is not easily explained or understood.

Nn

NAIL

A **nail** is a thin, sharp, pointed piece of metal used to join things. Farmer Brown fastens his wooden fences together with **nails**.
You also have a **nail** at the end of each of your fingers and toes.

NAME

What is your **name**? What are you called?
The dog's **name** is Digger. We call the dog Digger.

NAP

If you are tired during the day you take a **nap**. You have a short sleep. Baby Brother has a **nap** after lunch.

NAPKIN

A **napkin** is made of cloth or paper. It protects our clothes when we eat.
Nancy **Napkin** is made of linen.

NARROW

The stripes on Benjamin Butcher's apron are **narrow**.
They are not wide.

NATIVE

Zebby Zebra is a **native** of Africa. That is where he comes from.

NATURE

Anything in our world not made by man is part of **nature**.
The sea, sky, mountains, animals, birds and trees are all part of **nature**. They are **natural**.

NAUGHTY

Clarence Cat was **naughty** today. He was not good. He stole a fish from the table.

NAVY

The fleet of ships and all the people serving on them make up a country's **navy**.

NEAR

Nice Nurse lives **near** the hospital. She lives close to the hospital.

NEAT

Jenny keeps her room **neat**. She keeps it clean and tidy.

NECESSARY

Something that must be had or done is **necessary**.
It is **necessary** for Gilly Goldfish to have water in her bowl so that she can breathe.
She must have water in her bowl.

NECK

Your **neck** is the part of your body between your head and shoulders. George Giraffe's **neck** is very long.

NECKLACE

A string of beads worn round the neck is a **necklace**.
Aunty Ivy wears a pearl **necklace**.

NEED

We **need** to eat to give us energy. We must eat.
Andy Ambulance **needs** a siren. He has to have a siren.

NEEDLE

A **needle** is a thin piece of metal with a point at one end and a hole at the other to hold thread.
Belinda Ballerina uses a **needle** to sew the sequins on to her dress.

NEIGHBOUR

Mary lives next door to Joe.
She is Joe's **neighbour**.

NEITHER

Neither means not one and not the other of two.
Neither Jenny nor Jill is a boy.
They are both girls.

NEPHEW

Someone's **nephew** is the child of that person's brother or sister.
My **nephew**, Shaun, is my sister's son.
My **nephew**, Peter, is my brother's son.

NERVOUS

Missy Mouse is **nervous** of Clarence Cat.
She is afraid of Clarence Cat.

NEST

The bird built a **nest** in the tree.
This is its home.
It will lay its eggs in its **nest**.

NET

A **net** can be made of string or wire.
Farmer Brown has a wire **net** round his field.
When we play tennis we hit the ball to and fro over the **net**.

NEVER

Tilly Tortoise will **never** run as fast as Digger Dog.
At no time will she be able to run as fast as Digger Dog.

NEW

Baby Brother has a **new** toy.
It is not old: Mummy has just bought it from the shop.
Aunty Ivy has a **new** hairstyle.
She has a different hairstyle.

NEWSPAPER
News is printed in a **newspaper**. Tommy Teacher reads his **newspaper** each morning before going to school.

NOTICE

Did you **notice** Clarence Cat's sharp claws? Did you see them? Tommy Teacher pinned a **notice** on the wall. He wrote a message on a card and put it on the wall.

NEXT
Big Bus is parked **next** to Minnie Mini-Bus. They are side by side. Big Bus will be the **next** bus to leave the bus station. No other bus will go before he does.

NIGHT
Night is the dark time of day after sunset.
We go to bed at **night**.
The stars come out at **night**.

NOUGHT
Nought is the figure **0**.
If you take 5 away from 5 you have **0**.

NOVEMBER
November is the eleventh month of the year.
November has thirty days.

NOW
Now means at this moment.
I am reading this book **now**.

NICE
Daniel Dwarf is a **nice** man. He is a likeable man.
Jack and Jill had a **nice** time at the zoo. They had a very pleasant time at the zoo.

NIGHTDRESS

Belinda Ballerina wears a pretty **nightdress** when she goes to bed. Baby Brother wears pyjamas.

NUMBER

NIECE
Someone's **niece** is the daughter of that person's brother or sister.
My **niece**, Sharon, is my brother's daughter.
My **niece**, Julie, is my sister's daughter.

NOTHING
There is **nothing** left in Digger Dog's bowl.
It is empty. He has eaten everything.

A **number** is a figure not a letter and it tells you how much or how many of something.
Elly Elephant has 4 legs. 4 is the **number** of legs she has.

Oo

OAK

An **oak** is a type of tree.
The wood from **oak** trees is hard.
Acorns grow on **oak** trees.

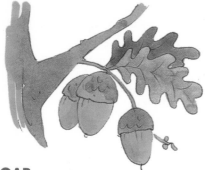

OAR

An **oar** is a flat blade of wood with a long handle. A boat can be rowed with two **oars**.

OATS

Farmer Brown grows **oats** on his farm.
When they are ripe he harvests them.
Filly Foal likes to eat **oats**.
We eat **oatmeal** made from **oats**.

OBEY

You should **obey** your parents and your teacher.
You should do what they tell you to.

OBJECT

An **object** is a thing. This book is an **object**.
Missy Mouse **objects** if Clarence Cat chases her. She does not like it.

OBLONG

An **oblong** is a shape which is longer than it is wide.
Some loaves of bread are **oblong-shaped**. Bricks are also **oblong**.

OCCASION

An **occasion** is a happening or an event.
A birthday is a special **occasion**.

OCEAN

An **ocean** is a large area of salt water. There are five **oceans** altogether. The Atlantic **Ocean** is one. Do you know the others?

O'CLOCK

O'clock is used in telling the time to say what hour it is.
Four **o'clock** is tea time.
Nine **o'clock** is the time school begins.

OCTOBER

October is the tenth month of the year.
There are thirty-one days in **October**.

OCTOPUS

An **octopus** lives in the sea. It has eight long arms, or tentacles, with suckers which it uses to catch its food.

OF

Of means belonging to or made from.
Nancy Napkin is made **of** linen.
Mother Goose is the mother **of** many children.

OMELETTE

An **omelette** is a kind of pancake. When Henrietta Hen lays some eggs we can use them to make an **omelette**.

ON

This word can tell you where things are or it can mean the opposite of off.
Digger Dog is sleeping **on** the settee.
Brian Baker must switch **on** the oven before he can bake his bread.

ONCE

Once means one time only.
Bobby Boy missed the school bus **once**. He missed it on one occasion only.

ONE

One is the first number. If you take 2 from 3 you have **1**.

ONION

An **onion** is a vegetable. It has a strong smell.
Chief Chef puts an **onion** in his casserole.

ONLY

Belinda Ballerina is an **only** child. She has no brothers or sisters.
Natalie Niece had **only** a sandwich for lunch. She had nothing else to eat for lunch.

OPEN

Nellie Neighbour's window is **open**. It is not shut.
Benjamin Butcher's shop is **open**. It is ready for the customers to come in.

OPERA

An **opera** is a play in which the words are sung instead of spoken. Perhaps Carol Canary could sing in **opera**.

OPPOSITE

Opposite means as different as possible or helps to tell you where something is.
Wet is the **opposite** of dry.
Fast is the **opposite** of slow.
The toyshop is **opposite** the post office.

OR

Or shows that there is a choice. Leo Lion can wear his red shorts **or** his blue shorts. He can wear either.

ORANGE

An **orange** is a juicy, round fruit that grows in hot countries. It is very good to eat.
Orange is a colour between red and yellow.

ORANG-UTAN

An **orang-utan** is a large ape from Borneo or Sumatra which lives in trees. **Orang-utans** have long arms, short legs and are covered in reddish-brown hair.

ORCHARD

Fruit trees grow in an **orchard**. Farmer Brown has a small field of apple, pear and plum trees. This is his **orchard**.

ORCHESTRA

An **orchestra** is a group of people who play music together. Lots of different instruments make up an **orchestra**.

ORGAN

An **organ** is a very large, musical instrument, often found in a church. It has keys rather like a piano.

ORPHAN

Norman Nephew is an **orphan**. Both his mother and father have died.

OSTRICH

Ossie is an **ostrich**. He is a large bird from Africa. He can run very fast but he cannot fly.

OTHER

Are there any **other** passengers waiting for Big Bus?
Are there any more passengers waiting for Big Bus?
I will go home by the **other** road.
I will take a different way home.

OTTER

An **otter** is an animal which lives by rivers or lakes.
An **otter** swims very well and feeds on fish.

OVER

Over can mean above, covering or finished. Kathy Kangaroo jumped **over** the fence. Natalie Niece often wears a sweater **over** her blouse.
The game was **over**. It had finished.

OWE

Jack **owes** Jill fifty pence. He has borrowed the money from Jill and must pay it back.

OWL

An **owl** is a bird. An **owl** has big eyes and flies mostly at night.

OWN

To **own** something is to have or possess something.
Farmer Brown **owns** his farm. It is his property.

OX

An **ox** is a large, farm animal. In some countries **oxen** are used for pulling carts or ploughs.

OYSTER

An **oyster** is a type of shellfish. The shell of an **oyster** may contain a pearl.

Pp

PACK

A group of wolves is called a **pack** of wolves.
Nellie Neighbour **packs** her clothes when she goes on holiday.
She puts them all in a bag.

PAD

A **pad** can be a cushion.
Bouncing Baby has a **pad** on his bed to make it soft.
Several sheets of paper fastened together make a different kind of **pad**.

PADDLE

People **paddle** in the sea when they are on holiday.
They walk in shallow water.

A **paddle** is a short pole with a flat end which is used to move a canoe through the water.

PAGE

A **page** is a sheet of paper in a book or a magazine.
This book contains lots of **pages**.

PAIL

Farmer Brown carries water to his animals in a **pail**.
He fills a bucket with water and takes it to his animals.

PAIN

Uncle Harry has a **pain** in his head.
His head hurts. It is **painful**.

PAINT

Nellie Neighbour is going to **paint** her door green. She will colour her door with a green liquid.

PANCAKE

A **pancake** is good to eat.
It is made from flour, milk and eggs and is cooked in a frying pan.

PANDA

A **panda** is a large animal rather like a bear.
The giant **panda** is black and white and comes from China.

PANTOMIME

A **pantomime** is usually performed at Christmas-time. It is a play which tells a fairy story.
Cinderella is my favourite **pantomime**.

PAPER

Paper is used to write on. Exercise books are made of **paper**.
This book is made of **paper**.

PARACHUTE

Uncle Harry used a **parachute** when he jumped from Arnold Aircraft.
A **parachute** was fastened to his body and when it opened he floated to the ground.

PARADE

Jack and Jill marched in the **parade**.
A band played music and lots of people **paraded** through the town.

PARCEL

The postman brought the boy a big **parcel** on his birthday. He brought a package wrapped in paper and tied with string.

PATIENT

Nice Nurse cares for **patients** in her hospital. She looks after people who are sick.

PATTERN

Nellie Neighbour made a dress using a **pattern**. She used the **pattern** as a guide. She likes the pretty **pattern** on her material. She likes the design.

PAW

A **paw** is the foot of an animal. It has claws on it.
Digger Dog and Clarence Cat each have four **paws**.

PAY

Nellie Neighbour must **pay** Benjamin Butcher when she buys her meat from his shop. She must give him money in exchange for the meat.

PEA

Farmer Brown grows **peas** on his farm.
Pea seeds are round and green and good to eat. They grow in pods on the **pea** plant.

PEBBLE

A **pebble** is a small stone. Bobby Boy collected some **pebbles** on the beach and used them to decorate his sandcastle.

PEDESTRIAN

When Jenny walks down the street she is a **pedestrian**. She must cross the road at a **pedestrian-crossing**. She must cross at a special place for people on foot.

PEEL

Albert Ape must **peel** the banana before he eats it. He must take the skin off.

PENGUIN

Peter **Penguin** lives near the South Pole. He is a black and white bird who lives near the water. **Penguins** cannot fly. They swim well and eat fish.

PEOPLE

Big Bus carries lots of **people** on his journeys. He carries men, women and children.

PEPPER

Pepper is used for flavouring food. It tastes hot.
Mother adds some **pepper** to the stew to give it more flavour.

PERFUME

The roses in Aunty Ivy's garden have a pleasant **perfume**. They smell good.

PERHAPS

Perhaps means possibly or maybe.
Perhaps Clarence Cat will catch a mouse. Clarence Cat might catch a mouse.

PERMISSION

Brian Baker gave Jenny **permission** to take a cake. He allowed her to take a cake.

PERSON

Benjamin Butcher is a **person**. Nellie Neighbour is a **person**. A **person** is a human being.

PHOTOGRAPH

Photographs are pictures taken with a camera. People often take **photographs** of each other.

PIANO

A **piano** is a large musical instrument with a keyboard. Do you have a **piano** at your home?

PICTURE

Bobby Boy drew a **picture** of Digger Dog. He drew a likeness of Digger Dog.
Aunty Ivy has lots of **pictures** on her walls.

PIECE

Bobby Boy eats a **piece** of cake. He eats a part of the cake.

PIG

Piggles **Pig** lives in a sty on Farmer Brown's farm. He has four short legs and a curly tail.
Ham and pork come from **pigs**.

POEM

Can you write a **poem**?
A **poem** is a piece of writing usually in rhyme.

PONY

A **pony** is a small horse.
Farmer Brown has a **pony** for the children to ride.

POTATO

A **potato** is a vegetable which grows below the ground.
We make chips from **potatoes**.

PRAWN

A **prawn** is a type of shellfish and lives in water.
Do you like **prawn** cocktail?

PRESENT

A **present** is a gift.
Belinda Ballerina received lots of **presents** on her birthday.

PRICE

What is the **price** of that bicycle in the shop window? How much does it cost?
The **price** of something is the amount of money it costs.

PROMISE

To **promise** is to say you will do something and to do it.
Bobby Boy **promised** to tidy his own room so he had to do it.

PUPIL

A **pupil** is somebody who is being taught.
Tommy Teacher has lots of **pupils** at his school.

PURSE

Aunty Ivy keeps her money in a **purse**.
A **purse** is a small bag for carrying money.

PUSH

To **push** is to use force to move something forward.
Mother has to **push** Bouncing Baby's pram to make it move.

PUT

Nice Nurse will **put** a vase of flowers on the patient's table.
She will place a vase of flowers on the table.

PYJAMAS

Do you wear **pyjamas** to sleep in?
Bobby Boy is wearing his **pyjamas**. He has a thin jacket and trousers, of the same material, to wear in bed.

Qq

QUACK
"**Quack!**" is what Daffy Duck says.
Quacking is the sound made by ducks.

QUARREL
John and Jane had a **quarrel**.
They had an argument.

QUARTER
A **quarter** is one of four equal parts of anything.
Brian Baker cut the cake into four equal parts.
He cut it into **quarters**.

QUEEN
A **queen** is a woman who rules over a country.
The wife of a king is called a **queen**.

QUESTION
How old are you? That is a **question**.
A **question** asks for information.

QUEUE
There is a **queue** at Benjamin Butcher's shop. There is a line of people waiting to be served.

QUICK
Nellie Neighbour must be **quick** if she wants to catch the bus.
She must hurry.

QUIET
Bobby Boy must be **quiet** or he will wake Bouncing Baby.

QUILT
Uncle Harry has a **quilt** on his bed.
He has a padded covering which keeps him warm.

QUIT
To **quit** is to stop or give up.
Naughty Norman Nephew **quit** school.
He stopped going to school.

QUITE
Brian Baker's cakes are **quite** delicious. They are really delicious.
Baby Brother has been **quite** good today. He has been really good.

QUIZ
Tommy Teacher organised a **quiz** at school. He held a competition and asked his pupils questions.

Rr

RABBIT

A **rabbit** is a small animal with soft fur. Reginald **Rabbit** has long ears and lives in a burrow.

RACE

A **race** is a competition to see who can go the fastest.
You can have **races** on foot, or car, horse and bicycle **races**.

RADIO

Aunty Ivy likes listening to music on her **radio**.
A **radio** is a piece of equipment for sending and receiving sound waves.

RAG

Mother cleans her oven with a **rag**.
She uses a piece of old cloth.

RAIL

A **rail** is a bar of wood or metal. Farmer Brown has a wooden **rail** fence around his fields.
Tracy Train runs on steel **rails**.

RAIN

Mother Goose hopes it will not **rain** today because she has hung her washing out to dry.
When it **rains** drops of water fall from the clouds.

RAINBOW

A **rainbow** appears in the sky when the sun shines through rain.
A **rainbow** is an arch of seven colours and is very pretty.

RAINCOAT

Uncle Harry will wear his **raincoat** because it is raining. He will not get wet because a **raincoat** is a waterproof coat.

RAISE

Tommy Teacher told the children to **raise** their hands if they knew the answer to his question.
He told them to lift up their hands.

RAKE

A **rake** is a long-handled, gardening tool for gathering up leaves or grass.

RAT

Raymond **Rat** looks like a large mouse. A **rat** is an animal with a long tail and sharp teeth.

RATHER

Bobby Boy would **rather** watch television than go to bed. He prefers to watch television.
It is **rather** cold today.
It is quite cold today.

READ

To **read** is to look at words and understand what they mean. You are **reading** this book.

READY

Dinner is **ready**. Dinner is cooked and on the table or prepared for you to eat.
Nellie Neighbour is **ready** to go out.
She has her coat on and is about to go out.

REAL

Real means true and not imagined. Digger Dog is a **real** dog. He is a proper dog and not a toy.

REAR

Uncle Harry sat at the **rear** of the bus.
He sat at the back of the bus.

REASON

Nice Nurse was late for work because she missed the bus.
That is the **reason** she was late.

RECEIVE

Bobby Boy is happy to **receive** a present on his birthday.
To **receive** is to accept something that is given.

RECOGNISE

Benjamin Butcher will **recognise** his regular customers. He will know them because he has seen them before.

RECTANGLE

A **rectangle** is a shape with four straight sides of two different lengths. All the corners of a **rectangle** are always right angles. Tommy Teacher has drawn a **rectangle** on the blackboard.

RED

Red is a colour. Some apples are **red**. Do you like **red** apples or green apples?

REMAIN

Baby Brother must **remain** at home. He must stay at home because he has a bad cold.

REMEMBER

Remember to take your books to school in the morning.
Do not forget them.
Did you **remember** to clean your teeth this morning?

REMOVE

Farmer Brown must **remove** his muddy boots before he goes into the house. He must take them off.

RENT

Nellie Neighbour pays **rent** for the use of her house.
She pays money to the person who owns her house.

RESTAURANT

A **restaurant** is a place where meals are served.
Chief Chef cooks meals in a **restaurant**.

RETURN

You must **return** to school on Monday after the weekend break.
You must go back to school on Monday.

RHINOCEROS

A **rhinoceros** is a large animal with a thick skin. **Rhinoceroses** come from Africa or Asia.
Ronnie **Rhinoceros** has one horn on his nose but others may have two.

RICH

Farmer Brown is **rich**. He has lots of money.
If you saved all your pocket-money you would be **rich** too.

RIDE

Bobby Boy can **ride** a bicycle.
He can travel along without falling off.
You can also **ride** on a horse or **ride** in a bus.

RIGHT

Do you know the **right** answer?
Do you know the correct answer?
Jack writes with his **right** hand but Jill writes with her left hand.

RING

Nellie Neighbour wears a **ring** on her finger. The **ring** is a circle of gold.
Did you hear the bell **ring**? Did you hear the sound of the bell?

RIPE

The banana is **ripe**. It is not green but yellow and ready to eat.

ROAST

Granny **roasts** meat in the oven.
She cooks it in the oven.
Do you prefer **roast** beef or **roast** chicken for dinner?

ROBIN

A **robin** is a small, brown bird with a red breast.
Look at Red **Robin** sitting on Dad's spade.

ROOT

All plants have **roots**. The **root** is the part which grows under the ground. Water is taken in through the **roots**.

ROPE

A **rope** is a thick string.
Farmer Brown ties a **rope** to Gertie Goat's collar to lead her to the field.

ROSE

A **rose** is a pretty flower which grows on a bush.
Roses have thorns on their stems.

ROTTEN

The apples at the bottom of the barrel were **rotten**.
They had gone bad and were not fit to eat.

ROUGH

The sea is **rough** today. It is not calm.
Elly Elephant's skin is **rough**. It is not smooth.

ROUND

Round means shaped like a ball or a circle.
Round things roll easily.

ROUTE

When we go on holiday, Dad plans our **route** very carefully. He plans which roads we should take.

ROW

Uncle Harry planted a **row** of potatoes in his garden. He planted them in a neat line.
Dad **rows** his boat across the river. He moves it along with the oars.

RUB

To slide something backwards and forwards against something else is to **rub**.
Dad **rubs** his hands together to warm them when he is cold.

RUBBER

Rubber is made from the sap of a tropical tree. Lots of things are made of **rubber**, for example tyres and erasers.

RUN

When you **run** you move with much quicker steps than you do when you walk.
Jack can **run** faster than Jill.

RUNWAY

A **runway** is a level strip of land especially for the use of aeroplanes. Arnold Aircraft takes off and lands on a **runway**.

RUSH

To **rush** means to hurry. The children **rush** home from school so that they can go out to play.

RYE

Rye is a grain which is used for feeding to animals.
Whisky and bread can also be made from **rye**.

Ss

SACK

A **sack** is a large bag in which we carry things.
Farmer Brown is carrying a **sack** of corn.
Chief Chef bought a **sack** of potatoes.

SADDLE

A **saddle** is a seat.
We sit on a **saddle** when we go for a ride on a horse or a bicycle.

SAFE

Safe means free from harm or danger.
You are **safe** when a policeman helps you cross the street.

SALT

Salt is a white, grainy substance found in the ground and in sea water.
We sprinkle **salt** on food to make it taste better.

SAME

Same means just like.
Bobby Boy's ball is the **same** as Baby Brother's ball.
It is the **same** size and the **same** colour.

SAND

Sand is tiny grains of worn-down rock found on the seashore or in deserts.
Baby Brother likes to play in the **sand** on the seashore.

SATCHEL

A **satchel** is a small bag.
Bobby Boy carries his books in a **satchel** when he goes to school.

SATURDAY

Saturday is the seventh day of the week.
Saturday comes after Friday.

SAVE

When you **save** your pocket money you keep it to spend later. Firemen often **save** people from danger. They rescue people from burning buildings.

SAW

A **saw** is a tool for cutting wood and metal.
A **saw** has a thin, metal blade with sharp teeth.
Norman Nephew used a **saw** to cut down an old tree.

SCISSORS

Scissors have two sharp blades that are fastened in the middle. We use **scissors** to cut paper and cloth. Barry Barber cuts Baby Brother's hair with **scissors**.

SEA

The **sea** is salt water that covers a large part of the earth's surface.
Wally Whale and Flipper Fish swim in the **sea**.

SEAL

Sammy **Seal** is a sea animal with furry skin. **Seals** have flippers to help them swim.

SEASON

A **season** is one quarter of a year.
Spring, summer, autumn and winter are the four **seasons** of the year.

SEAT

A **seat** is a thing to sit on.
Chairs, stools, benches and sofas are all **seats**.

SECOND

The **second** is the one after the first.
Elly Elephant came first in the race and Daniel Dwarf came **second**.
A **second** is also a short period of time.
There are sixty **seconds** in a minute.

SECRET

A **secret** is something only you know until you choose to tell other people about it.
Digger Dog hides his bones in a **secret** place.

SEE

We **see** with our eyes.
What do you see on this page?
Eric Elf went to **see** Daniel Dwarf last Saturday. He went to visit him.

SEED

A **seed** is that part of a plant which can grow into another plant.
Aunty Ivy plants **seeds** in her garden.
Farmer Brown plants grass and vegetable **seeds** in his fields.

SELL

If you **sell** something you hand it over in exchange for money.
Benjamin Butcher **sells** meat.
Brian Baker **sells** bread and cakes.

SEND

To **send** is to cause something or someone to move from one place to another.
Bobby Boy will **send** Aunty Ivy a present at Christmas.
Mother will **send** Baby Brother to bed if he is ill and then she will **send** for the doctor.

SENTENCE

A **sentence** is a group of words that tell or ask something.
Can you read this **sentence**?
Sidney Ship sails on the sea.

SEPTEMBER

September is the ninth month of the year.
There are thirty days in **September**.

SERVE

Mother will **serve** the food.
She will wait on us and give us our share.

SHADOW

A **shadow** is a patch of shade. Anything blocking the light from the sun casts its own **shadow**. Wherever you go your **shadow** goes with you.

SET

Please **set** the room straight. Put everything in its proper place.
Doc Doctor can **set** a broken bone.
Mother Goose **set** the table for the party.
Bobby Boy **set** the alarm for seven o'clock.

SEVEN

Seven is the number after six.
Seven is one more than six.
There are **seven** days in a week.
6 + 1 = 7.

SEVENTEEN

Seventeen is the number after sixteen.
Seventeen is seven more than ten.
10 + 7 = 17.

SEW

To **sew** is to fasten cloth together with stitches.
We **sew** using a needle and thread. We can **sew** by hand or by using a **sewing** machine.

SHAKE

To **shake** something is to move it up and down, or from side to side, quickly.
The two boys **shake** the tree to get the apples.

SHALLOW

The water is **shallow**. It is not deep. It is usually safe to paddle in **shallow** water.

SHORT

Short means not long or tall.
The boy has **short** hair but Natalie Niece has long hair.
Dad is tall but Baby Brother is **short**.

SHOULDER

A **shoulder** is the place where the arm of a person, or the front leg of an animal, joins the body.
Bobby Boy carries his satchel on his **shoulder**.

SHOW

Jack will **show** Jill the photograph he took of her. He will let her see it.
A **Show** can be a competition for animals or birds.
Digger Dog hopes to win a prize at the Dog **Show**.

SHUT

To **shut** is to close something. You **shut** your eyes when you go to sleep.
We **shut** doors, windows and gates.

SIXTEEN

Sixteen is the number after fifteen.
Sixteen is six more than ten.
$10 + 6 = 16$.

SIZE

Size means how big or how little
something is.
Aunty Ivy grows flowers of all sizes,
big and little.
Tilly Tortoise is larger in size than
Snowy Snail.

SKI

A ski is one
of a pair of
long, thin
pieces of
metal
fastened to
the underside
of boots for
gliding over
snow.
To ski is to
travel over snow on skis.
Bobby Boy's ambition is to ski down
a mountain.

SKY

The sky is the space above the
earth. At night the sky is dark.
During the day the sky looks blue.
We see the sun, the moon and the
stars in the sky.
Arnold Aircraft flies in the sky.

SLEEP

We shut our eyes when we go to
sleep. We rest our minds and our
bodies when we go to sleep.
When we sleep we are not awake.
People, animals and birds sleep.

SLEEVE

A sleeve is that part of a dress,
jacket or coat which covers part or
all of the arm.
Belinda Ballerina's dress has short
sleeves.
Farmer Brown's jacket has long
sleeves.

SLIPPER

A slipper is a soft, comfortable
shoe that we wear indoors.
Baby Brother has a pair of warm,
woollen slippers.

SLOW

Snowy Snail takes a long time to get

to the party because he is a slow-
moving creature. He cannot go
fast.
Sometimes a road sign warns drivers
to slow down because there is
danger ahead.

SMALL

Missy Mouse is small. She is not
large like Elly Elephant.
Baby Brother is small. He is not big
or tall.

SMILE

Bobby Boy has a smile on his face.
He has a happy look on his face
because he has found his ball.

SNAIL

Snowy Snail is a small animal with
a coiled shell in which he can hide
when danger threatens.
Snowy Snail moves very slowly.
Snails live in water or on land.

SNOW

Snow is soft, white flakes of frozen
water which fall from the sky in
winter.
The children will build a snowman
from the snow that lies on the
ground.

SOON

Tracy Train will come **soon**. She will come in a short time. Bouncing Baby must go to bed **soon**. He must go to bed before long.

SORRY

The children are very **sorry** that David is ill. They feel sad that he is ill. Snowy Snail said, "I am **sorry** I am late but I cannot go any faster."

SOUND

Any noise is a **sound**. We hear **sounds** with our ears. Sh! Do not make a **sound**. Bouncing Baby is asleep.

SOUP

Soup is a liquid food made by boiling meat, or fish, or vegetables in water. Uncle Harry likes beef and vegetable **soup**.

SOUTH

South is a direction. When you face the rising sun in the east, **south** is to the right. **South** is opposite to north.

SPADE

A **spade** is a tool for digging. A **spade** has a blade and a handle. Father digs the garden with a **spade**. Baby Brother likes to dig in the sand on the shore with his little **spade**.

SPELL

To **spell** is to write or say the letters of a word in the right order. S U N spells sun. A **spell** is a short period of time. In winter we have **spells** of snow. A **spell** can also be a magic charm cast by a fairy, or a witch, or a wizard. Some **spells** are good; some are evil.

SPIDER

Spikey **Spider** is a small animal with eight legs and no wings. **Spiders** spin webs to catch insects for food.

SPRING

Spring is the first season of the year. A **spring** is a small trickle of water coming from the earth. To **spring** is to leap or jump. Will Clarence Cat **spring** at Missy Mouse?

SQUARE

A **square** is a shape with four sides that are the same length. The spaces on a chessboard are **squares**.

SQUIRREL

A **squirrel** is a small animal with grey, red or dark brown fur and a long, bushy tail. Squeaky **Squirrel** lives in a tree and eats nuts. He stores away nuts to eat in winter.

STABLE

A **stable** is a building where horses are kept and fed. Filly Foal lives in a **stable**.

STAMP

A **stamp** is a small piece of printed, gummed paper to be stuck on parcels or envelopes so the Post Office will send them where we want them to go. If you **stamp** your feet you bang them on the ground.

STREET

A street is a road in a town or city that usually has shops and houses on both sides.
Traffic travels along the street so you must be careful when you cross a street.

STRING

String is thick thread, or thin cord, rope or wire.
We tie packages with string.
Vicky Violin has four strings made of thin wire.
Baby Brother uses a string to fly his kite.
A number of things in a line or row is called a string.
A string of racehorses galloped down the track.

STRIPE

A stripe is a long, narrow band.
Tiggy Tiger has stripes.
Zebby Zebra has black and white stripes.
Benjamin Butcher has an apron with blue and white stripes.

SUDDEN

Sudden means quick and unexpected.
A sudden noise woke Bouncing Baby.

SUGAR

Sugar is what we put in food to make it sweet. Sugar is made from the juice of sugar cane or sugar beet.

SUMMER

Summer is the warmest season of the year and comes between spring and autumn.

SUN

The sun is the brightest object in the sky. The sun shines during the day and gives us light and heat.
The earth travels round the sun once every 365¼ days.

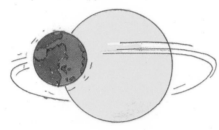

SUNDAY

Sunday is the first day of the week.
Sunday comes after Saturday.

SUPERMARKET

A supermarket is a large, self-service shop which sells food and household goods.

SWAN

A swan is a large water-bird with short legs and a long, curving neck.

SWEATER

A sweater is a warm garment worn on the upper part of the body. Aunty Ivy is knitting a sweater for Bobby Boy.

SWEEP

To sweep means to brush with a broom to make something clean.
Natalie Niece likes to sweep the floor.
Bobby Boy will sweep the path.

SWEET

Things that taste like sugar or honey are sweet.
Sweet also means charming or pleasant.
Bouncing Baby is a sweet child.
Some flowers have a sweet smell.

SWIM

To swim is to make your body move through water. People swim by moving their arms and legs.
Daffy Duck and Gracie Gosling swim with their feet.
Fish swim by moving their fins and tails.

Tt

TABLE

A **table** is a piece of furniture with a smooth, flat top on legs.
A list of facts and figures is also called a **table**. Bobby Boy learned the multiplication **tables**.

TACK

A **tack** is a short, pointed nail with a broad, flat head.
Farmer Brown used **tacks** to fasten the sign to the fence.

TADPOLE

A **tadpole** is a baby frog. It hatches from frogs' spawn and has to live in water. Then it grows legs and can go on land as a frog.

TAG

A **tag** is a small label tied to a thing to tell something about it.
In a game of **tag** one person chases the others until he touches one of them who then does the chasing.

TALK

When we **talk** we say something.
Aunty Ivy likes to **talk** about the flowers in her garden.

TALL

Tall is high.
George Giraffe is a **tall** animal.
A sky-scraper is a **tall** building.
Father is a **tall** man but he is not as **tall** as Geoffrey Giant.

TAME

Some animals are **tame**. They are no longer wild but have become gentle and used to being with people.
Some birds are so **tame** they will take food from your hand.

TANK

A **tank** is a large container used to hold liquid or gas.
Big Bus has a petrol **tank**.
Timmy **Tank** is an armoured, military vehicle with caterpillar tracks so he can travel over rough ground.

TASK

A **task** is a piece of work that has to be done.
Bobby Boy's **task** is to feed Digger Dog each day.

TASTE

We use our tongues to **taste** the flavour of food or drink.
Baby Brother likes the sweet **taste** of ice cream.

TEA

Tea is a hot drink made by pouring boiling water over the dried and shredded leaves of the **tea** plant.
Some people put milk and sugar in **tea** to make it taste sweet.

THEATRE

A **theatre** is a building where plays are acted.
The children went to a **theatre** to watch the pantomime.

THEY

They is used to refer to people, or animals or things.
Albert Ape and Mickey Monkey are friends. **They** like each other.

THIRSTY

If you are **thirsty** you want a drink. Bouncing Baby drinks milk when he is **thirsty**.

THIRTEEN

The number **thirteen** is one more than twelve. 12 + 1 = **13**.
Thirteen is three more than ten. 10 + 3 = **13**.

THIS

THEIR

Their means belonging to them. The children brush **their** hair and clean **their** teeth and shine **their** shoes before they go to school.

THICK

Thick means not thin. We wear **thick** clothes in cold weather. A **thick** liquid is hard to pour.
Thick also means set close together. Dainty Doll has **thick** hair.

THIEF

A **thief** is someone who steals. **Thieves** take things which belong to other people.

THEN

Then means at that time, or next, or soon after.
The party begins at four o' clock. Will you be there **then**?
The lightning flashed and **then** we heard the thunder.

THERE

There means not here but in, or at, or to, some other place.
The park is over **there**. They have swings and roundabouts **there**. Do you want to go **there**?

THIN

Thin means not fat or thick. Belinda Ballerina is **thin** but Piggles Pig is fat.
We wear **thin** clothes in hot weather.
Spikey Spider hung from a **thin** thread.

This refers to the person or thing near to you or just spoken about.
This is my friend. We shall go for a walk **this** morning. Shall we go **this** way or that?

THORN

Thorns are sharp points that grow on the stems of some plants. Rose bushes have **thorns**.
Dad tore his sleeve on a **thorn**.

THUMB

The **thumb** is the shortest and thickest of the five end parts of your hand.
Bouncing Baby sucks his **thumb** when he is tired.

THUNDER

Thunder is the loud noise which usually follows a flash of lightning during a storm.

THURSDAY

Thursday is the fifth day of the week.
Thursday comes after Wednesday.

TICKET

A **ticket** is a piece of paper or card which shows the price of something.
You buy a **ticket** to see a show or to travel somewhere.

TOGETHER

Together means with each other.
Daniel Dwarf and Eric Elf play **together**.
Farmer Brown put all his cows **together** in one field.

TOMATO

A **tomato** is a juicy red or yellow fruit with many seeds.
Tomatoes are good to eat with lettuce and cucumber.

TOMORROW

Tomorrow is the day after today.
If today is Wednesday, **tomorrow** will be Thursday.

TONGUE

A **tongue** is the soft, movable, piece of flesh in the mouth used for tasting and eating and, by people, for speaking.
Frankie Frog catches flies with his long **tongue**.

TOO

Too means also or as well.
Bouncing Baby is tired and hungry **too**.
Too also means more than enough.
Elly Elephant ate **too** much.

TOOL

A **tool** is anything that is used in doing work.
A spade is a **tool** for digging.
A pen is a **tool** for writing.
A saw is a **tool** for cutting wood.

TOOTH

A **tooth** is one of the hard, white, pointed parts that grow in the mouths of people and most animals. They are used for biting and chewing and you should clean your **teeth** every day.
Christopher Crocodile has very sharp **teeth**.

TOP

The **top** of something is its highest point or part.
Albert Ape and Champ Chimp climbed to the **top** of the tree.
A **top** is a toy that spins round.

TORN

If something is **torn** it has a tear or rip in it.
Dad's sleeve is **torn**. He **tore** it on a sharp thorn.

TORTOISE

Tilly **Tortoise** is a slow-moving animal who lives on land.
Tilly **Tortoise** has a hard, thick shell on her back.

TOUCH

To **touch** is to feel something with any part of your body but usually your fingers or hand.
Do not **touch** Nellie Neighbour's door because the paint is still wet.

TOW

To **tow** is to pull or drag something along with a chain or rope.
Baby Brother likes to **tow** his toy train along the path.

TOY

A **toy** is something with which to play.
Most children like to play with **toys**.

TRACK

A **track** is a mark left by the movement of a person, animal or thing.
Bobby Boy's skis left a **track** in the snow.
Trains run on railway **tracks**.
A rough road or path is also called a **track** and so is a roadway or path used especially for racing.

TRAFFIC

Traffic means the coming and going of people and vehicles along a land, sea or air route.
It is dangerous to cross a street when there is a lot of **traffic**.

TRAIN

A **train** is a line of railway coaches or carriages pulled by an engine.

TRAINERS

Trainers are shoes with flat, rubber soles. Bobby Boy can run very fast when he is wearing **trainers**.

TRANSPORT

To **transport** people or things means to take them from one place to another. Passengers and goods can be **transported** by road, rail, sea and air.

TRAVEL

To **travel** is to make a journey or to go from place to place.
Arnold Aircraft hopes to **travel** round the world.

TRAY

A **tray** is a flat piece of metal, wood or plastic with a shallow rim round it that is used for carrying things.
Chief Chef carried a bowl of hot soup on a **tray**.

TROUSERS

Trousers are clothing worn over the legs, reaching from the waist to the knees or ankles.
Baby Brother wears short **trousers**.
Dad wears long **trousers**.

TRUCK

A **truck** is a large vehicle that carries things from place to place.
Farmer Brown uses a **truck** to transport his corn to the mill.

TRUNK

A **trunk** is a large box used for holding or carrying belongings.
An elephant's nose is also called a **trunk**. Elly Elephant picks up food and water with her **trunk**.
The main stem or body of anything is called a **trunk**. Trigger Tree has a thick **trunk**.

TRUTH

The **truth** is what is true, real or a fact.
We should always tell the **truth** because it is wrong to lie and liars usually get into trouble.

TRY

To **try** is to make an attempt to do something.
Bobby Boy will **try** to find his ball.
Try also means to test or give a trial to something.
Try these trainers to see if they fit.

TUESDAY

Tuesday is the third day of the week.
Tuesday comes after Monday.

TWELVE

The number **twelve** is one more than eleven. 11 + 1 = **12**.
There are **twelve** months in a year.

TWENTY

The number **twenty** is one more than nineteen. 19 + 1 = **20**.
Two tens make **twenty**.
2 x 10 = **20**.

TWIN

A **twin** is one of the two children or animals born to the same mother at one time.
Twins sometimes look alike.

TWINKLE

To **twinkle** is to shine and sparkle with quick flashes of light. Stars **twinkle** in the night sky.
Dad's eyes **twinkle** when he laughs.

TWIST

To **twist** is to wind or turn or to bend a thing out of shape.
Aunty Ivy **twists** her ring on her finger.
This path **twists** through the trees.

TWO

The number **two** is one more than one.
1 + 1 = **2**.
We have **two** hands and **two** thumbs.
Birds have **two** wings.

TYPEWRITER

A **typewriter** is a machine which prints letters and figures on paper when the keys on the keyboard are pressed individually.
A person who uses a **typewriter** is called a typist.

TYRE

A **tyre** is an air-inflated, rubber tube which fits round the rim of a wheel.
Nice Nurse cannot ride her bicycle because the front **tyre** has a puncture.

Uu

UGLY

If something is **ugly** it is not pretty to look at.
In some fairy stories witches and trolls have **ugly** faces. Do you know the story of the **ugly** duckling who became a beautiful swan?

UMBRELLA

An **umbrella** is a cloth-covered, metal frame on a stick you hold over your head to shelter you from the rain.
Umberto **Umbrella** is shaped like a mushroom but can fold up.

UNCLE

My father's brother is my **uncle**.
My mother's brother is my **uncle**.
My aunt's husband is my **uncle** too.

UNDER

Under is below or less than.
Clarence Cat hides **under** the bed.
Submarines can sail **under** the water.
The storm lasted **under** five minutes.

UNHAPPY

If you are **unhappy** you feel sad.
Bobby Boy was **unhappy** when he lost his ball.
David was **unhappy** when he was ill.

UNTIE

To **untie** means to undo or unfasten.
Some knots are easy to **untie**.
Remember to **untie** your shoe-laces before you take off your shoes.

UNTIL

Until means up to the time of or to the time when.
Farmer Brown works from morning **until** night.
Bobby Boy played football **until** dinner was ready.

UP

Up means on high, or to go to a higher place, or to be at or near the top. Squeaky Squirrel is **up** his tree.
Arnold Aircraft flew **up** into the sky.

UPON

Upon means on the top of something.
Put the plates **upon** the shelf and the cups **upon** the table.

UPSTAIRS

Upstairs means not on the ground floor, or beyond a staircase.
Bobby Boy sleeps **upstairs**.
Dad walked **upstairs** from the cellar.

USE

To **use** is to make something do a job of work for some purpose.
We **use** a knife to cut things.
We **use** our minds to think.

USUAL

Usual means what often happens or something done so often it is well-known.
Nice Nurse had her **usual** happy smile on her face.
It is **usual** for Bouncing Baby to drink milk.
Daniel Dwarf met Eric Elf at their **usual** meeting place.

Vv

VACANT

Vacant means empty and unoccupied.
That house is **vacant**. Nobody lives there and there is nothing inside.

VACATION

A **vacation** is a holiday.
Bobby Boy had a week's **vacation** from school, so Uncle Harry took a week's **vacation** from work. They spent their **vacation** at the seaside.

VALENTINE

A **valentine** is a card or a gift for someone you love which is sent to them on **St Valentine's Day**, February 14th.

VALLEY

A **valley** is the low land that lies between two hills or mountains.
Some **valleys** have rivers or streams running through them.

VALUE

Value means the price, importance, or usefulness of something.
What is the **value** of Aunty Ivy's gold ring?
Healthy people recognise the **value** of regular exercise.

VARNISH

Varnish is a sticky liquid that is painted on a surface to protect it.
It dries to a hard, shiny surface.
Natalie Niece puts pink **varnish** on her finger nails.
The floors at Tommy Teacher's school are covered with **varnish**.

VASE

A **vase** can be used as an ornament or for holding flowers.
Aunty Ivy put some red roses in a pretty, blue **vase**.

VEGETABLE

A **vegetable** is a plant that we grow for food and which is not a fruit.
Peas, beans, lettuces, potatoes, carrots, cabbages and onions are **vegetables**

VEHICLE

A **vehicle** is a car, wagon, lorry, bus, cart, or sleigh, or any other means used for carrying goods or people from place to place on land.
Andy Ambulance, Jonty Jeep and Timmy Tank are **vehicles**.

VEIL

A **veil** is a piece of very thin material worn over the head or face as part of a head-dress.
Dainty Doll has a **veil** on her favourite hat.
A **veil** can also be worn to hide or protect the face.

VERSE

Verse is another name for poetry.
A **verse** is a group of lines from a song or poem, or a short section from a chapter in the Bible.
Do you know the first **verse** of 'Mary Had a Little Lamb'?

VERY

Very means extremely.
It is **very** cold today.
Mother Goose is always **very** busy.

VIEW

To **view** means to look at.
Farmer Brown likes to **view** his
fields from the top of the hill.
The scene, or all that he sees before
him, is called a **view**.

VILLAGE

A **village** is a group of houses,
sometimes with a church or shops,
that is much smaller than a town.

VINEGAR

Vinegar is a sour liquid made from
apples or grapes and is used for
flavouring and pickling food.

VIOLIN

Vicky **Violin** is a small musical
instrument with four strings played
with a bow or sometimes by
plucking.
A **violin** is held
under the chin
when it is
being
played.

VISIT

To **visit** is to go or come to see
someone or something.
Percy Peacock will **visit** his friend
Peter Penguin.
Daffy Duck and Lucy Lamb **visited**
the circus last week.
A **visit** is also a short stay.

VITAMIN

A **vitamin** is any of a number of
special substances found in food that
are needed to make our bodies
strong and healthy. **Vitamins** are
named after letters of the alphabet.
Oranges contain **vitamin C**.
Vitamins are found especially in
raw fruits and vegetables, fish, milk,
butter and cereals.

VOICE

Your **voice** is the sound from your
mouth when you speak or sing.
The referee's **voice** was loud.
Natalie Niece likes singing because
she has a sweet singing **voice**.

VOLCANO

A **volcano** is a mountain with an
opening at the top, called a crater,
through which steam, gases and hot
melted rock are thrown out.

VOLUME

Volume is the amount of space
something occupies or the amount of
room inside it. The **volume** of a
house is more than the **volume** of a
dog kennel. What is the **volume** of
your toy-box?
A **volume** is also a book, or one of
a set of books.
Bobby Boy owns several **volumes**.

VOTE

A **vote** is your stated choice or wish
in a matter that concerns you.
People **vote** by raising a hand, by
speaking, or by writing on a piece of
paper called a ballot paper.
The team **voted** for Bobby Boy to
be captain.

VOYAGE

A **voyage** is a journey by sea or
air.
To **voyage** is to travel or make a
journey, especially to a far-away
place.
Sidney Ship's **voyage** across the
ocean will take five days.

VOWEL

The letters a, e, i, o, u, and sometimes y, are **vowels**. There are five
vowels in the word mysterious.

Ww

WADDLE

To **waddle** is to walk with short steps and rock from side to side. Daffy Duck and Goosey Gander both **waddle**.

WADE

To **wade** is to walk through water. Do you like to **wade** in the sea?

WAFER

A **wafer** is a very thin, crisp biscuit. We usually eat **wafers** with ice-cream.

WAG

Digger Dog **wags** his tail when he is happy. He moves his tail from side to side.

WATCH

A **watch** is a small clock that can be worn on the wrist, carried in a pocket or worn on one's clothing. To **watch** means to look at something.
Bobby Boy likes to **watch** his kite fly high in the sky.

WATER

Living things cannot survive without **water**. It is the liquid that fills the oceans, seas, rivers, lakes and ponds. Rain is **water**.
To **water** is to put **water** on plants or to give animals **water** to drink.

WATERFALL

A **waterfall** is a stream of water falling from a high place.

WAVE

A **wave** is a line of moving water rising and falling on the surface of the sea.
Sidney Ship was tossed by **waves**. If you **wave** to someone you move your hand to and fro. Brian Baker **waved** to Aunty Ivy as she passed.

WAX

Wax is the soft, yellowish substance bees make to use for honeycombs.
Beeswax and other similar substances are used to make candles and polish.

WEAR

To **wear** a thing is to have it on your body. We **wear** warm clothing in cold weather. Nellie Neighbour **wears** a gold ring on her finger. **Wear** also means to rub away or damage through use. Dad walked to work and **wore** a hole in his shoe.

WEATHER

Weather is how hot, cold, wet or still the air is outside at any one time or place.
The air is warm in hot **weather**.

WEDDING

A **wedding** is a ceremony at which a man and a woman are married and so become husband and wife.

WEDNESDAY

Wednesday is the fourth day of the week.
Wednesday comes after Tuesday.

WELLINGTONS

Wellingtons are knee-high, rubber boots for keeping our feet dry in wet weather.

WERE

We use the word **were** when we talk about more than one thing in the past.

The children **were** playing in the garden and **were** late for school.

Those trees **were** once small but now they are tall.

WEST

West is the direction opposite to east. The sun sets in the **west**.

WET

Wet means soaked or covered with water or other liquid.

Digger Dog got **wet** in the rain.

Wet also means not yet dry.

The ink is still **wet**.

WHALE

A **whale** is a huge, sea animal that is shaped like a fish. Some **whales** are larger than any other animal in the world.

WHAT

What is a word we use when asking questions. **What** time is it? **What** would you like to do today? **What** also means that which and anything that.

If you know **what** you want you may take it and I will keep **what** is left.

WHEAT

Wheat is a plant that produces the grain from which flour and bread, as well as many breakfast cereals, are made. Farmer Brown grows **wheat**.

WHEEL

A **wheel** is a round frame that turns on its axle or centre.

Wheels help things move more easily.

Big Bus, Trevor Tractor and Tracy Train all run on **wheels**.

WHEELBARROW

A **wheelbarrow** is a small cart with a single wheel at the front, two legs at the back and two handles to lift so that it can easily be pushed along.

Wheely **Wheelbarrow** carries small loads.

WHEN

When means at what time or at the time that.

When does the party begin? It will start **when** the guests arrive.

WHERE

Where means in or at what place.

Where does Digger Dog sleep?

Where shall we meet?

Where also means to or from what place.

Where are you going now?

Where did you get that book?

WHICH

Which means what one or that.

Which girl won the race?

Choose the book **which** you like best.

WHITE

White is the colour of fresh snow. Nice Nurse wears a **white** apron. Brock Badger has a **white** face with two black stripes.

WHO

We use the word **who** when asking about people.
Who is your best friend?
Who is coming to the party?
Who also means that.
The boy **who** whistled is my cousin.

WHOLE

Whole means complete with nothing missing or broken.
Aunty Ivy bought a **whole** set of dishes at the market.
The **whole** family watched Piggles Pig eat a **whole** pie.

WHOM

Whom means what person or which people. **Whom** do you like best?
To **whom** shall I send these invitations?

WINDMILL

A **windmill** is a mill with fanlike sails on top which are pushed round by the wind to grind corn or to pump water or to generate electricity.

WINDOW

A **window** is an opening in a wall or roof of a building to let in light or air or to provide a view.
Windows are usually filled with glass or clear plastic.
Ships, trains, cars and many other vehicles have **windows**.

WINTER

Winter is the fourth season of the year coming after autumn and before spring.

WIRE

Wire is a bendable strand or thread of metal which has many uses.
Cages and fences are often made of **wire**.
When you telephone someone your voice travels through a telephone **wire**. **Wires** carry electricity to where it is needed.

WITNESS

If you see something happen you **witness** it. The policeman **witnessed** the accident.
A **witness** gives evidence at a trial in a court of law and takes an oath to tell the truth about what he or she has seen.

WOLF

A **wolf** is a wild animal, very much like a large dog, that lives and hunts in packs. **Wolves** can be very fierce and greedy.

WOMAN

A **woman** is a grown-up, female person. Aunty Ivy is a **woman**. Natalie Niece will be a **woman** when she grows up.

WOOD

Wood is the solid part of a tree under the bark and is used for making houses, furniture, boats and many other things.
Vicky Violin is made of **wood**.

WORD

A **word** is a group of letters so arranged that they have a meaning. **Words** can be written or spoken. Have you read all the **words** in this dictionary?
Speak up! I didn't hear a **word**.

WORK

Work is the effort needed to make or do anything. **Work** is also employment in a job. Nice Nurse **works** in a hospital.

WORLD

The **world** is the earth and everything there is on it.
The **world** is round.
Some ships sail round the **world**.

WORM

A **worm** is a long, thin, legless animal that lives in the ground.
Birds like to eat **worms**.

WORRY

To **worry** is to feel anxious or troubled. If you are late coming home your parents will **worry**.

WORSE

Worse means something not as good as something else or that something is not being done as well as before.
Eric Elf was quite ill yesterday but he is **worse** today.
The tap is dripping **worse** than ever.

WORTH

A thing of **worth** has value, importance or usefulness.
What is Aunty Ivy's necklace **worth**?
Good health is **worth** more than great wealth.
A saw has to be sharp to be of any **worth**.

WOULD

Would means wished to or was willing or determined to do something.
Bobby Boy said he **would** feed Digger Dog.
Snowy Snail **would** go to the party even though he was feeling ill.

WRING

To **wring** is to twist and squeeze hard.
Wring out your wet clothes and hang them up to dry.

WRIST

The **wrist** is the joint where the hand joins the arm.
Uncle Harry wears a watch on his left **wrist**.
Natalie Niece wears a bracelet on her right **wrist**.

WRITE

When we **write** we put letters, words, or figures on paper, or some other surface, so that they can be read.
Bobby Boy has **written** a letter and now he will **write** a story.

WRONG

Wrong means not right or good. It is **wrong** to steal or to cheat or to tell lies.
Wrong also means not true or correct.
Bobby Boy gave a **wrong** answer.
That is the **wrong** way to fly a kite.

Xx Yy Zz

XMAS
Xmas is a short word for Christmas.
A sign in a shop said 'Merry **Xmas**'.

X-RAY
An **x-ray** is an invisible ray that can pass through solid things.
Special cameras use **x-rays** to take shadow photographs of our insides.
Doc Doctor studied the **x-ray** of Dad's broken leg.

XYLOPHONE
A **xylophone** is a musical instrument made of wood or metal bars, each of which gives a different note when struck with a small, wooden hammer.

YACHT
A **yacht** is a light, speedy boat with sails which is used for pleasure trips or racing.

YARD
A **yard** is an area of enclosed ground round or near a building which may be used for some special purpose.
Children play in the **school-yard**.
Sidney Ship was built in a **shipyard**.

YAWN
To **yawn** is to open your mouth wide and breathe out with a long, deep sigh when you are sleepy or bored.
Bouncing Baby **yawned** and fell asleep on Mother's lap.

YEAR
A **year** is the time it takes the earth to travel once round the sun.
There are 52 weeks, 12 months or 365¼ days in a **year** but 366 days in a Leap **Year** which comes every fourth **year**.

YEAST
Yeast is used in making bread.
When mixed in a sugary liquid, **yeast** becomes frothy and the air in the tiny bubbles makes the bread rise.

YELL
To **yell** is to scream, shout or cry out loudly because of pain, fear or excitement.
Daniel Dwarf **yelled** when he bruised his knee.
The team **yelled** when Bobby Boy scored the winning goal.

YELLOW
Yellow is a colour.
Carol Canary has **yellow** feathers.
Butter is **yellow**.
Bananas are **yellow**.

YES
Yes means the opposite of no.
Mother said, "**Yes**, you may go to the park."
We say '**Yes**' when we agree.
"**Yes**, there are seven days in a week," says Tommy Teacher.

YESTERDAY
Yesterday means the day before today.
If today is Saturday, **yesterday** was Friday.

YOGHURT

Yoghurt is a thick, creamy food made from milk. Fruit is sometimes added to **yoghurt** as a flavouring.

YOLK

The yellow part of an egg is called the **yolk**.

YOU

You means the person or persons being spoken to or written to.
Dad said, "If **you** yawn once more, **you** will go to bed."
The invitation said, "Will **you** come to my party?"

YOUNG

Young means not old or grown up.
Natalie Niece is a **young** girl.
Filly Foal is a **young** horse.
A sapling is a **young** tree.

YOURSELF

Yourself means just you and no-one else. You can see **yourself** if you look in the mirror.
Did you hurt **yourself** when you fell?

YOUTH

Youth is the time when a person is young. Tommy Teacher told the children tales of his **youth**.
The word **youth** can mean one young man like Bobby Boy or it can mean a group of young people. Natalie Niece is a member of a **youth** orchestra.

ZEBRA

A **zebra** is an African animal like a small horse. Zebby **Zebra** has black and white stripes all over his body.

ZERO

Zero is a number meaning nought, nothing or none at all and is written like this - **0**.
6 - 6 = **0**.
Zero is the point marked as **0** on a thermometer. If the temperature is **zero** it is very cold.

ZIP

A **zip** is a fastener made of two rows of metal or nylon teeth which is shut and opened by a sliding catch. Clothing, luggage and footwear are often fastened by means of **zips**.

ZODIAC

The **zodiac** is an imaginary belt in the heavens, along which the sun, moon and chief planets seem to move.
It is divided into twelve equal parts, named after groups of stars, called the Signs of the **Zodiac**.

ZONE

A **zone** is an area or region used for a particular purpose. A parking **zone** is where parking is permitted.
A **zone** is also any of the five great divisions of the earth's surface.
The Frigid **Zones** within the Arctic and Antarctic Circles are very cold.

ZOO

A **zoo** is where wild animals are kept for people to see and study them.
Albert Ape and George Giraffe are in the **zoo** too.